Bedtime Sleep Meditations For Children 2 In 1 Bundle

Guided Night Time Short Stories With Positive Affirmations To Help Kids & Toddlers Fall Into Deep Sleep At Night, Relax, And Have Beautiful Dreams

Author: Sleepy Willow

Copyright 2021 – All rights reserved.

The content contained within this book may not be reproduced, duplicated or transmitted without direct written permission from the author or the publisher.

Under no circumstances will any blame or legal responsibility be held against the publisher, or author, for any damages, reparation, or monetary loss due to the information contained within this book. Either directly or indirectly.

Legal Notice:

This book is copyright protected.

This book is only for personal use. You cannot amend, distribute, sell, use, quote or paraphrase any part, or content within this book, without the consent of the author or publisher.

Disclaimer Notice:

Please not the information contained within this document is for educational and entertainment purposes only.

No warranties of any kind are declared or implied. Readers acknowledge that the author is not engaging in the rendering of legal, financial, medical or professional advice.

The content within this book has been derived from various sources. Please consult a licensed professional before attempting any techniques outlined in this book.

By reading this document, the reader agrees that under no circumstances is the author responsible for any losses, direct or indirect, which are incurred as a result of the use of the information contained within this document, including, but not limited to: errors, omissions, or inaccuracies.

TABLE OF CONTENT

Bedtime Sleep Meditations For Kids

Introduction 1

Chapter 1 3
   Your Perfect Paradise 3

Chapter 2 21
   The Land Of Unicorns 21

Chapter 3 38
   Lovely Ocean Adventures 38

Chapter 4 71
   Magical Forest Friends 71

Chapter 5 95
   Positive Bedtime Affirmations 95

Conclusion 108

Bedtime Sleep Meditations For Children

Introduction 113

Chapter 1 115
    The Confident Mermaid Adventure 115

Chapter 2 126
    The Magic Carpet Ride 126

Chapter 3 135
    The Fairy Forest 135

Chapter 4 141
    Rapunzel And Believing 141

Chapter 5 151
    The Sleepy Animal Kingdom 151

Chapter 6 182
    The Magic Unicorn Adventure 182

Chapter 7 213
    Great Undersea Friends 213

Conclusion 222

Bedtime Sleep Meditations For Kids

Short Stories With Positive Affirmations To Help Children & Toddlers Fall Asleep At Night, Relax, And Have Beautiful Dreams

Author: Sleepy Willow

INTRODUCTION

Thank you for choosing *Bedtime Meditations For Kids*.

In this magical and wonderful book, you will be taken on many adventures and listen to wonderful stories that will help you to fall asleep peacefully every night. I hope that you and your children will have hours of fun reading these stories. Each story in this book will be entertaining and will have small lessons that your child can learn from. You will learn many skills that can help you relax your mind and body, so you have the most amazing sleep every night. Each story contains valuable lessons while relieving stress. Each story will empower you and your children to improve your self-confidence and self-esteem. You will learn how to deal with your emotions better and communicate them more effectively.

Children who experience lots of nightmares might be scared to fall asleep at night and might have a hard time relaxing at night because they are afraid of scary dreams. This book will help you combat and get rid of those fears. Each story will help you feel more relax, calm, loved and completely safe. You have nothing to worry about from now on.

After you have brushed your teeth, combed your hair and put on nice comfortable pajamas, it's time for you to snuggle down in bed and get ready for sleep. You can now pick any story to help you relax and drift off to an amazing sleep.

Make sure you read each story and follow along. Each story has a relaxing meditation to help you get cozy and comfortable for a good night's sleep.

Are you ready to begin your bedtime meditation stories? Choose any story to begin your adventure now!

CHAPTER 1

Your Perfect Paradise

Close your eyes and take a nice deep breath.
Allow your tummy to fill up like a balloon.
Then slowly exhale gently and smoothly.

Take another deep breath,
allowing your tummy to fill up like a balloon.
And slowly and gently exhale.
One more time take a nice big deep breath,
Allowing your tummy to fill up like a balloon.
The slowly and gently exhale,
And relax.

Now, imagine yourself in your bedroom.
You notice something is glimmering and shining on your bedroom wall.

You can see what it is,
And you are not scared of it at all.
In fact, you are drawn towards it,
and you feel quite excited.
As you begin to take a closer look at it,
It appears to be pulsing and shimmering like a thousand stars.
It seems to be some kind of portal into another world.

You extend and dip your hand in the portal and does not hurt at all.
In fact, it feels really nice.
It feels warm and soothing to the touch.
Can you feel it?
Now dip your head in and take a little peak on the other side.
Wow!
This is truly amazing!
It's is a portal to paradise.
In this paradise you can see all of your favorite things.
You can see theme parks, water parks, and you can even see flying unicorns.
What else can you see with all of your favorite things?

Now you fully walk through this portal, and you instantly feel happy.
You feel full of joy.
This paradise doesn't just have all of your favorite things,
But it also makes you feel amazing on the inside too.
A place where you can leave any worries and stresses behind you.
In this place, well you just feel happy.

You notice a welcome banner with your name on it.
This place is just for you.
You can invite anyone you want to it.
Spend some time now in your very own paradise.
Maybe you can take a ride on a unicorn.
Maybe you can play with fairies.
Maybe you can even take a ride on a waterslide.
You may even want to see a special person or a pet that you can no longer see in your normal life.
You decide this is your special place

In this place, it not only allows you to be around all of your favorite things,
It also allows you to see only the good and beauty in all things.
Even with the people you don't usually like.

Here you can see only the good in them.
You can see only the goodness all around you.
You can see the good and beauty in every situation.
Badness has no place here.
You can see the beauty in everything.
You can feel the beauty in everything.
Even the things you think are ordinary in everyday life like the leaves of a tree, or like the grass under your bare feet.
Can you see it?

Can you feel it?

It's now time to come back from this beautiful place.
So, you jump through the portal and return back to your room.
But you have now brought back with you all those feelings of joy and happiness.
Best of all you can return back to your portal of paradise whenever you like.

Now imagine you are walking towards the ocean.
Walking through a beautiful tropical forest.
You can see the trees around you are very tall, very elegant.

You can even smell the fresh clean air.
You can hear the sounds of all the different animals and birds in this forest.
Can you hear them?

You start to hear the waves from the ocean ahead of you.
You can hear the sound of them coming up under the sand on the beach.
You can even smell the ocean spray.
The lovely smell that you can only find at the beach.
Can you smell it?
You continue to walk along your path getting closer to the sea.
As you come to the edge of the trees,
You see the brilliant blue color of the ocean ahead.

You can hear the magnificent sound of the ocean waves.
They are so much louder now.
You walk out of the forest and onto a long stretch of glorious white sand.
The sand is very soft as you take off your shoes and your socks.
You walk through the warm white Sun rays towards the water.

You can feel the Sun beneath your feet and start to feel it between your toes.
Can you feel it?

This beach is very wide and very long.
It stretches for miles ahead.
You can hear the waves washing up onto the shore.
You can smell the colleen saltwater.
You can even smell the clean crisp air.
You look again at the ocean and it is the deepest and most beautiful blue you have ever seen.

Now imagine yourself walking toward the water.
Under the fine hot Sun, you're feeling a little hot now.
Just a little bit sticky too.
As you walk, you can see the sparkles of the sunshine dance upon the water's surface.
It's like a million tiny stars all shining and dancing just for you.
It looks so beautiful.
A wave washes over the Sun towards you and you can feel it touch your toes before gently receding.
As you step forward more waves wash over your feet.
It feels so cool and refreshing.
It is so calming and soothing on your feet.

You begin to walk a bit further into the clear clean water.
You can see the white foam under the water.
You can still feel the water between your toes.
Can you feel your toes squashed into the sand and wriggling them about in the water?

You can now see a few small fish swimming.
Fast positive flashes of color as they pass by.
The water is very pleasant and cool, but not too cold.
You walk a little further into the water,
And you decide you want to take a gentle swim.
So, enjoy the ocean for a few minutes.
Allow yourself to float and drift around in the beautiful deep blue ocean.
Just float around with all the little fish
And just relax.

Now, you are feeling very calm and refreshed.
You're feeling very peaceful and very very relaxed.
You walk out of the water and back onto the beach again.
Feeling again the soft sand beneath your feet and your toes.
You walk along the water's edge and you feel free of any worries you might have had.

All of your problems have been washed away,
And now you only feel very calm, very peaceful and so relaxed.
You turn around and you see a comfortable lounge chair and a towel just for you.
You go over and sit on the chair.
You like sitting on the chair and maybe
You may decide to spread the towel in the Sun and just relax on the chair.
Just relaxing and enjoying the sunshine and
The cool breeze upon your face.
The warmth of the sun on your skin.
The sound of the waves making you feel every so peaceful.
Making you fel every so happy just watching the waves
Rise and flow.
Backwards and forwards.
Backwards and forwards.
You feel so calm.
So calm so relaxed and very very peaceful.
You just sit there for a little while longer.
Enjoying the lovely relaxation that has been made just for you.
Now, it's time for you to return back to your normal life.
It's time to come back home now.
Imagine you're standing on a beach.

On your very own private magical island.
A place that's yours.
A place where you can relax and feel very safe.
This magical island of yours is surrounded by the bluest ocean.
The water sparkles and shines like a thousand diamonds glittering in the Sun.
Above your island is a rainbow of many colors.
Can you see it floating above your island?
Can you see it in the sky?

You turn and look into the distance and you see the tops of mountains.
Some of them reaching so high you can see snow on the very tips of them.
You start walking towards the amazing forest
and to the pathway that will lead you to these beautiful mountains.
You step onto the path and begin to walk.
You can hear birds singing.
Can you hear them?
You can see many flowers blooming in many colors.
You can hear the sounds of tiny animals rustling in the bushes as they go about their day.
You can't see them but you can hear them
Listen

Your pathway starts to rise now.
You can feel the muscles in your legs getting tighter as you walk.
Your heart begins to beat just a little bit faster.
Up ahead of you, you see an animal waiting for you.
It's your guide for the rest of your journey.
What animal can you see?
It is your favorite animal?
Or is it one you haven't seen before?
Your animal guide beckons for you to follow it.
So you do and the two of you walk in a very blissful silence.
So peaceful you think how nice it is to be with a friend.
A friend where it's ok if you don't talk.
It's okay just to be together happily walking along.
You can hear the birds singing their songs as they fly high above you.
You and your animal guide stop for a little rest.
You see a bench and the two of you sit on it for a little while.
Your animal guide sits beside you saying nothing at all.
The two of you just sit in a peaceful silence.
You spend a few moments just sitting and being still and quiet with your animal guide.
Look around you and just enjoy how peaceful it is hear and just listen.

Your journey to the top of the peaceful mountain with your guide ends now.

Your guide points you in the direction you need to go with a single light showing you the way.

This part of the journey you walk alone but that's okay,

Because you don't mind.

You feel so safe, so peaceful and fell so well protected.

You begin to walk.

You reach the top and find a very old stone village on the edge of the mountain.

You can see an old bridge with a gentle waterfall flowing back down the mountainside.

There is a beautiful garden just outside of the village walls.

You see a small group of people sitting in a circle on the ground.

One of them turns and welcomes you, but not with their voice.

With their thoughts and beautiful smile.

You walk over to them and take your place beside them in a circle.

Thoughts pop into your head telling you that you're with a tribe of very peacefull people.

People who don't talk.

They don't use their voices.
They are all wearing white robes
And they give you one to put on.
You feel like you've been here before.
It feels like home to you.
It's so peaceful here.
You have never felt so at peace.
You know in your heart that just by being you will never feela lone again.
These are the people of silence.
Their language is silence.
You don't even have to hear their thoughts.
You just know what they are telling you.
You can feel it through the silence.
You learn so much more truth than anything else because
you can feel the truth in your heart.
This really makes your soul sing with happiness and peace.
You look around and see beautiful vistas all around the top of the mountain.
You really do know that you will never be alone again.
You finally realize that everything is perfect just the way it is,
as you sit there atop the mountain.
You feel so big,
You feel so connected and apart of everything.

You feel as one with the world and with these people of silence.
You realize that all of the answers to your questions can be found in this beautiful silence.
Its makes you feels so at peace.
You also know that the only time these wonderful beings use their voices is when they sing.
When they sing it's like angels are talking to you.
These beautiful people of silence know that to sing is to connect to your heart.
The people of silence begin to sing.

Can you hear it?

Can you feel it?

You have never heard anything like it before.
These words touch your heart in a way that you have never felt before.
It really does make your soul sing with complete and utter joy.
Listen even closer.
What can you hear?

What can you feel with your soul?
You become totally immersed in this beautiful song.
It's almost like a soulful lullaby tempting you to sleep.

So, sit for a little while in silence with these amazing people.
Just listen.
Lay your head on the soft and gentle grass.
If sleep comes calling just listen and remember.
You can return any time you wish,
and spend time with the people of silence and just listen.

Now imagine there is a tiny door in the back of your mind.
On that door there is a sign and it says sleeping mind.
Can you see it?
Can you see the sign?
You open the door and enter the most beautiful bedroom.
This is your favorite room.
Inside this bedroom you can have anything you want.
All of your favorite things to help you relax and feel safe.
This is your room and it can be any way you want it to be.
Anything that makes you feel happy and relaxed.
You can have any kind of bed you want.
It can be a great big bed or it can be a bed that looks like a racing car.

It can be a bed that's surrounded with unicorns to help you sleep.

It can even be a bed that is just a cloud and it floats above your floor.

Anything you want you can have.

Even your favorite teddy bear or toy can be there with you.

This wonderful bed of yours can have the most amazing fluffy pillows for you to lay your head on, and the softest quilt to keep you warm and help you snuggle down.

This room is the perfect temperature for you, just the way you like it.

There is a lovely scent of lavender flowers drifting around the room.

You don't know where its coming from, but it smells lovely and relaxing.

The only sound you can hear is the perfect and gentle music.

It's very soft in the background.

So very peaceful.

You really like it as you listen to the sounds of the music.

You realize that nobody can disturb you in your peaceful place.

This peaceful place with your sleepy mind.

This is a place to let go all your thoughts.

All your worries because they don't matter here.

It's very safe and you will only ever feel happy and sleepy when you are here.
So, for a few moments create your perfect bedroom in your mind.
Create all the things that bring you peace.
Make it look just how you want it to be.

Now that you have the most perfect bedroom,
you climb upon your perfect bed.
You lay your head upon the soft and fluffy pillows.
You give a great big sigh of happiness.
You look over to the large window with beautiful curtains hanging on either side of it.
Through this window you can see the night sky,
and the beautiful stars shining like diamonds glittering so brightly.
You stare at them for a few minutes and imagine that you can see lots of other beds just floating high above you in the night sky.
Each of those beds has someone in them just like you all gently drifting off to sleep.
So now if you like, you can leave the curtains open and sleep by the light of the stars.
Or you can use your own mind and slowly close them and shut out the stars to get ready for sleep.
It's so peaceful, calm and quiet in your mind now.
Just enjoy it.

Your eyes are feeling really heavy now.
Your body is feeling so very tired.
You take a deep breath in through your nose and gently blow it out from your mouth.
You take another deep breath and gently blow it out from your mouth.
You're feeling very sleepy now.
So tired and relaxed.
You feel a gently wave of sleepiness starting at your feet.
It's a warm and gently feeling.
Kind of like how a feather feels when you brush it against your skin.
So soft and gently.
You can feel your toes going to sleep.
It feels warm and tingly ever so soft.
You feel the soothing gently wave of sleepiness going up your calves and your shins.
You can feel it going up your thighs.
You think your legs have already gone to sleep.
You feel very tired now.
So sleepy.
So happy.
It feels like you can't open your eyes, but that's okay.
You don't need to open your eyes.

This beautiful wave of sleepiness travels all the way up your body, down your arms and into your hands, making you body feel very very heavy.
Very very tired and very very sleepy.
This gently warm wave of sleepiness travels up your face and over the top of your head, down the back of your neck.
You feel so tired, so sleepy now.
You feel nice and warm and snuggly under the soft quilt and your very fluffy pillow.
Just have a little sleep now.
I am going to count from 5 to 1.
Remember the time we get to 1 you'll be asleep are you ready?

5
You feel so sleepy.
4
So tired for feeling warm and safe.
3
Feeling so protected.
2
Feeling so very very safe.
1

Feeling so very very loved.
Night night.
Sleep tight.

CHAPTER 2

The Land of Unicorns

Close your eyes and make yourself comfortable.
Take a deep breath in through your nose.
The slowly and gently breathe out through your mouth.

Again, take another deep breath in through your nose.
Then slowly and gently breath through your mouth.
One more time, deep breath in.
And slowly and gently breathe out through your mouth.

Now bring your breathing back to its normal rhythm.
Feeling your chest rise and fall gently.

Feeling peaceful and calm.
Feeling very relaxed.
With each breath you take, you can feel yourself becoming more and more relaxed.
Your body feels quite floppy and you feel so peaceful now.
So relaxed and yet you feel very happy and very light.
Your breathing is almost still.
You are so relaxed.

Now, imagine yourself sitting in a large green field.
The sun is shining brightly and it's a very beautiful clear day.
You can see for miles and miles.
You feel very calm, very relaxed and ever so peaceful.
You can hear birds singing to each other.
Can you hear them?
As you look up at the sky, you see a beautiful rainbow of many colors.
The colors are so bright and so clear.
Can you see it?
Can you see how the colors sparkle and shine?
Can you see how the colors look almost alive?
You feel so drawn to this amazing rainbow that you walk towards it.

As you do, you feel your steps becoming lighter and lighter.

It's almost as if you are floating towards the rainbow.

It feels like your feet are not even touching the ground.

You stopped at the beginning of the rainbow.

You take a good look at it, and you realized the rainbow is actually moving.

It's actually a moving walkway.

Oh my goodness!

The rainbow stops moving and you step onto it.

As soon as you step onto it, the rainbow begins to move again.

As it moves forward it also begins to climb.

It climbs higher and higher.

You can even touch the colors of this rainbow.

What does it feel like to touch the rainbow?

The rainbow goes higher still.

You can now see the field below you.

You can see many trees.

You can see the birds flying.

There are even a couple of birds flying past your rainbow.

Can you see them?
The rainbow reaches the topmost part and begins to move back down again.
Now it's starting to get a bit slippy, so you sit down.
As you do, you begin to slide down.

Oh dear! You are sliding down the rainbow.
The rainbow is like a great big waterslide with beautiful colors all around you.
You are going faster and faster.
The wind is whipping through your hair making it fly everywhere.
This makes you laugh out loud.
You are laughing so hard that your tummy starts to hurt!

You can see the end of the rainbow and it's coming fast.
You notice that at the bottom of the rainbow, there appears to be a huge trampoline.
Oh my! You hit the trampoline so fast that you bounce right back up again.
Then back down, then right back up again.
This is so much fun!
So, you keep bouncing for a few minutes, up and down, up and down.

With each bounce, you see in the distance beautiful colors that you haven't seen before.
You can see many many fields and mountains.
You can see beautiful flowers too.
You've never seen them before either.
It's absolutely breathtaking to see such beauty.
You can also see what looks like horses in the distance, but they horns.
What cant be right.
Not unicorns surely no.
They can't be unicorns can they?
You stop bouncing and jump off the trampoline.
Go and investigate.
Go and see if they are really unicorns.
You start walking when you come across a huge sign and it says welcome to Unicornia, Land of The Unicorns.
Wow!
You look around you and you see unicorns everywhere!
There are large unicorns, there are small baby unicorns, there are unicorns all over the place!
Each and every one of them has a very special spiral horn on its head.
You move very quietly and very softly because you don't want to scare any of them away.
You don't want to frighten them.

You needn't worry because they are not scared of you at all.
In fact, they come up to you and say hello.
Yes, these beautiful and special beings couldn't talk.
They are very magical beings and they always know the truth og things.
The unicorns all speak at once.
They want to know your name.
They want to know how you got here, because only special good-hearted people can find the rainbow to Unicornia.

All of a sudden, the unicorns all stop talking and bow their heads.
A very different unicorn comes out from the rest of them.
This unicorn is very very beautiful.
She is much whiter than the others and her coat is very silky and very shiny.
She is a sparkling, glittering, magical unicorn and she looks about he same age as you.
You notice she has a diamond encrusted spiral horn with pink crystals on top of her head.
She has a beautiful silver mane with speckles of pink in it and beautiful silvers.
This magnificent unicorn walked so softly her hooves make no sounds.

Her spiral horn is the most powerful of them all.
Her spiral horn has the strongest healing qualities and it is magnificent.
The gentle breeze blows her across her spiral horn it produces a beautiful flute like melody.
It sounds so wonderful to you.
This unicorn is the princess of unicornia.
She is very special indeed.
She is a symbol of purity and grace.
She is such a powerful being and all she wants is for everyone to have peace and harmony in their life.

The princess unicorn speaks to you.
She tells you that magic is real.
She tells you that you must always believe in yourself,
and that you are so very special.
She is very gentle and loving, and you can feel the love she has for you.
She loves all beings.
She loves each and every one of us equally no matter how different we may look from each other.
She only sees the beautiful person we truly are.

The princess unicorn askes you if you would like to ride on her back.

Well of course you say yes.
She bows down for you to climb up, and when you are settled she starts to move.
For a few moments, you ride on the back of this majestic being.
Listen to what she has to tell you.
This magnificent place is unicornia.

The princess unicorn stops in front of these massive steps.
On these steps at the top, you see many beautiful crystals.
You climb down off her back.
She tells you to come up the steps with her.
As you walk up the steps you see that right in front of you is a beautiful crystal palace.
It shines and sparkles in the sunlight.
It is so beautiful and so magnificent.
The princess unicorn leads you up to the doors and two rather small elves open the doors.
You step inside and it is absolutely beautiful.
The princess unicorn asks if you like to around the palace and see how the live.
Would you like to see the princess's own bedroom?
You say "Oh yes please, this is wonderful."
The princess unicorn leads you up the great big stairs.

She is so excited she wants to take you to her bedroom first.
You go up with her and for a little while explore this beautiful palace.
You meet her family but most of all you see her bedroom.
What exciting things she has in there.
Just for a little while longer be in the palace.

Now it's time for you to return to your own home.
It's time for you to leave unicornia.
You thank the princess for all her kindness and for all that she has done for you today.
The princess tells you that you can come back here anytime you want.
There are many more things for you to visit.
There are many more beings for you to make friends with.
Before you go she asks you to touch her beautiful spiral horn.
As you do you feel a tiny shock.
It doesn't hurt. It just makes you jump a little.
You can feel a warm tingling sensation coming form her beautiful horn.
The princess unicorn tells you that she is sending her healing power to you.
Her healing power is in her beautiful spiral horn.

Any problems or worries that you may have had, is now being helped from the princess.
She is helping you overcome any difficulties that you may have.
She says she will be your best friend forever.
This makes you so happy you thank her for helping you.
You say goodbye.
You say goodbye to all the beautiful magical unicorns.
You turn to go.
The unicorn teaches us to believe in ourselves and in the reality of magic.
Remember those who don't believe in magic will never find it.
So, take a deep breath in.
Slowly and gently breathe out.
Deep breath in and slowly and gently breathe out.
One last time, deep breath in and slowly and gently breathe out.
Now, wiggle your fingers and wiggle your toes.
Slowly and gently open your eyes.

Find a place where you can sit, lay down, relax and not be disturbed.
Maybe in your bedroom or on your sofa.

Now, I want you to take a deep breath in through your nose.
And slowly and gently breathe out through your mouth again.
Deep breath in, and slowly and gently breathe out through your mouth.
One more time, deep breathe in and slowly and gently breathe out through your mouth.
Now just relax and let your breathing come back to its normal rhythm.

Now, I want you to imagine that you roots sprouting our from the soles of your feet.
Very strong, very noble roots.

They look like roots from a tree.
You can hear your roots growing through the ground.
You can hear them as they push their way through the soil.
Can you hear it?
Can you feel the soil under your feet all squishy?

Now imagine a beautiful white light surrounding your whole body.

A light so bright, that you shine brighter than a thousand suns.
It doesn't hurt you to look at it.
This beautiful white light is protecting you.

Now, imagine you are standing on your favorite beach.
A beach with golden sand.
You can feel the warm sun.
Sand beneath your bare feet and in between your toes.
Can you feel the sun tickling your feet?
Can you feel how warm it is?
Can you hear the sound of the ocean waves as they gently wash up on the sand?
You can even smell the salty air.
Can you smell it?
If you stick your tongue out, you can even taste it.
Try it.
Try and taste the salty air.
Stick your tongue out.
Can you taste it?

In the distance something catches your eye.
You squint your eyes to see what is moving towards you.

You are not afraid though because there is nothing here to be afraid of.

This is your special place and only you can say who comes to this place because it's yours.

You can now see what is coming towards you.

It is five unicorns.

Wow!

They stop in front of you and let you stroke them.

They are all truly beautiful creatures all soft and shiny.

Each unicorn is a different color.

Each of them have a gold and sparkling horn in the center of their head.

It glitters in the sunlight.

What colors are your unicorns? Can you feel their silky coats?

These are you own special unicorns that can take you on wonderful adventures.

With them you can co to far off lands.

You can see many different villages and see how other people live.

You can do to the desert if you want.

You can see the pyramids.

You can climb the highest mountain.

Where would you like to go?

What would you like to see?

One of the unicorns bows to their knees for you so that you can climb on their back.
You now climb up in its back.

It's your unicorn.
Male or female.
You wonder if they have a name, so you ask them.
You wait for them to whisper to you.
You unicorn asks where you want to go so you whisper it in their ear.

The unicorns all move as if they were one.
You hold on tight to the main as they start to trot.
You start to jiggle a bit as they move a bit quicker.
You feel very peaceful and calm on the back of your unicorn.
You feel excited and very happy.
You can feel the wind on your face.
You can feel the wind rushing through your hair.
You look up towards the sky and see the beautiful warm sun shining down on you.
It feels really lovely on your skin.

As your unicorn gallops forward have a look around you.
What do you see?

Do you see fields and trees?
Or do you see the ocean again?
What do you see?

You feels o happy riding on the back of your unicorn.
So peaceful and free.
You notice that all five of the unicorns all move exactly at the same time.
They are never out of step with each other.
They are so I harmony with each other that when you unicorn, who is in the front, moves a just a tiny bit, they all move exactly the same way, at exactly the same time.
You see up ahead a cliff edge, and you wonder why your unicorns are not slowing down.
All of a sudden each one of them grows beautiful gold and silver wings.
As they keep galloping faster and faster, they rise into the air higher and higher.
They go soaring up into the clouds.
Do you realize that you are flying?
They are flying!
You feel so amazing, so joyful and so happy.
You are flying.

You look around you and you see fluffy white clouds everywhere.

You and your unicorns fly around for a while.
Doing all that you see, so be free and just fly with your unicorns.

Your unicorns start to dive downwards now back through the clouds.
You can feel the tremendous rush of air on your face.
You can feel your clothes blowing in the wind.
You look beneath you and see the glorious countryside below you.
What else do you see?
You and your unicorns are flying over the fields and hills.
Racing past tall trees swaying in the breeze.
You feel so happy.
You feel so alive.
How does it feel to be so free?

Keep flying for as long as you wish.
Maybe you can ask your unicorn a question.
Is there anything you would like to ask your unicorn?

Now it's time to return home.
Just whisper in your unicorn's ear and ask them to take you home.

Whenever you feel ready to open your eyes just wiggle your fingers and toes.
Have a big stretch and then slowly and gently open your eyes.

Close your eyes now and make yourself comfortable.
Take a deep breath in through your nose.
And slowly and gently breathe out through your mouth.
Take another deep breath in and slowly and gently breathe out.

CHAPTER 3

Lovely Ocean Adventures

Settle yourself down into your lovely cozy bed.
We'll begin now.
First tense up all of your muscles and hold it for a few seconds.
Hold it tightly and let go allowing your arms and legs to nice and limp.
Now breathe in deeply really filling up your lungs with air.
Really fill them up.
Now breathe out slowly and gently.
Releasing all the air from your lungs.
Now breathe in again slowly and deeply.
And hold your breath for just a moment.
Hold your breath.

And breathe out.

Draw in another deep breath.
Hold the breath.

And breathe out.
Breathe in.
And breathe out.
Breathe in.
And breathe out.
Every time you breathe in you become more and more relaxed.
You can feel your body becoming very loose, very soft.
Now imagine you are walking along a beautiful white sandy beach.
The sand is very soft so you take off your shoes and your socks.
You walk on the warm white sand.
You can feel the sun beneath your feet.
Can you feel it between your toes?
Can you feel it?
Can you feel the sand flick up against the back of your legs?
The beach is wide and long.
It stretches for miles ahead.

At the far end of the beach you can see what looks like a lovely wooden cabin.
You walk towards it to go and see it.
As you walk you hear the sounds of the waves.
You can hear the sounds of them coming up and onto the sand.
You can even smell the ocean spray.
That lovely smell you can only find at the beach.
The ocean is a deep brilliant blue color and it sparkles in the sunshine.
It's like the waves are dancing just for you.
You can hear the magnificent sounds of the ocean waves so much louder now.
You can still hear the waves coming onto the shore.
You can smell the clean salty water.
You can even smell the sand.
You look out at the ocean.
It is the deepest blue you have ever seen.
As you reach what you thought was a cabin, you realize it's actually a beautiful white villa.
It's so pretty.
It has lovely big glass windows with window boxes.
There are butterflies dancing all around the flowers.
It has a little wrap around porch with a big swinging chair filled with soft cushions.
It looks very inviting.
You decide you want to go inside and see what it's like.

You gently tap on the door but there is no answer.
You tap again.
Still no answer.
So, you decide to go inside anyway.

You enter into a big lovely room filled with huge cushions, kind of like beanbags.
They are so big and the room is so bright and inviting.
You realize that all of the cushions are in a big circle.
You walk over to have a look and you give a little gasp for what you see.
The reason the cushions are in a big circle is because the lovely little white wooden villa has a glass floor.
It is very thick glass.
The kind of glass that doesn't break when you walk on it.
You take a seat on one of the soft cushions and take a look through the glass floor below you.
This is amazing!
Wow!
You can see the ocean below you.
The beautiful turquoise ocean.
You can see the water gently moving backwards and forwards.
As it flows in and out like the waves.

You see beautiful tiny little fish swimming by all glistening with color.
The colors are amazing so vivid and bright.
You see bigger fish again with bright dazzling colors.

They take no notice of you whatsoever.
They are just happily swimming along doing fishy things you know they like to do.
You can an eel smoothly gliding by.
The most amazing thing about this eel it has a tiny red top hat.
It looks kind of cool too.
It's kind of mesmerizing looking through the glass.
You wonder what else is swimming down below you.
What other delights are in store in the beautiful blue ocean.

You decide to stay here for a while and just watch the ocean.
It is teeming with all kinds of life.
You can even see the ocean floor.
You can see little crabs scurrying along in the sand.
One of them suddenly stops and looks up at you.
It looks like he's kind of smiling at you.
Surely crabs don't smile, do they?

He lifts up one of his claws and gives you wave and suddenly he curries off again.

Oh my! A crab just waved at you!

You give a little laugh.

As you watch some more you notice how kind all of the little creatures are.

They are helping each other to do things.

One little fish is helping another little fish move a rock out of the way.

Then you see the eel with the red top hat, come along too help .

He uses his nose and he just pushes the rock.

They are all so kind to each other.

This is so much fun to watch.

You can hear the crashing of the lapping of the ocean waves in this beautiful tropical paradise.

It sounds so peaceful and it's so calming and restful being here in this white wooden villa.

You think to yourself you would like to stay here forever and ever and ever.

So, settle yourself down on your very big soft cushion, and for a few moments just enjoy watching the undersea world.

See what else you can see.

See if there are any mysterious creatures that maybe you've never seen before.

If you like you can imagine yourself being under the water with them.

You can imagine breathing underwater just like the fish do.

Or maybe you prefer just to watch and learn about life under the sea right where you are on your big soft beanbag.

You have seen some amazing things in the water below you.

I really really enjoyed being here, but you realized now that you're feeling a bit sleepy.

So, you snuggle down even deeper in your big soft cushion.

You can still see the creatures below you.

You can still hear the sound of the ocean waves as they gently begin to lull you into a deep sleep.

Your eyes begin to feel heavy.

You find that your eyelids are beginning to droop.

Oh your body feels so peaceful.

So relaxed.

So calm and so very very heavy now.

You love being here in this beautiful tropical paradise.

It's so wonderful.

Just before your eyes begin to close, you see once again the little crab scurrying past.
And again he stops and looks at you and gives you a wave with his claw and then scurries off again.
You smile at him and think how lucky you are.

How lucky you are to be in such a beautiful place.
How lucky you are to be able to see how life is under the ocean waves.
You have seen how peaceful they live.
They all do live so peacefully together.
You have seen how they all help each other.
How kind they are to each other.
You think that kindness is a very wonderful thing.
You decide that from now on, you are going to be kind to everyone.

You close your eyes and just listen to the sounds of the ocean.
You can feel your breathing as it begins to slow down.
You feel your chest is just rising and falling very gently.
You listen to the rhythm of the waves as they gently begin to lull you into a beautiful and restful sleep.

Just listen to the waves as you go deeper and deeper into a sleep.
Feeling so peaceful so calm.

So relaxed and when you wake up in the morning, you will feel so refreshed and so very very happy.
You can always visit the little white wooden villa any time you want.

Now imagine you are on the most beautiful beach in the world.
The glorious white sand.
You can see trees on this beach but they are further back.
There's no one else there.
Just you.
You take off your shoes and your socks.
You walk along the sand and it feels nice and warm.
You can feel the sand beneath your toes.
You look ahead and you see a small clump of trees like palm trees.
You see a few rocks.
You think to yourself; I think I'll just go and have a sit down and look.
Just look around.
What can you see?

You see an odd bird flying past.
You see a few beautiful white fluffy clouds in the sky.
You see the most beautiful deep blue ocean.
You can hear the sounds of the waves as they come gently to the shore.
As you get nearer to this little clump of trees with a few big rocks, you wonder where these rocks came from.
There are no other rocks on the beach at all.
Just beautiful white sand.
You reach the little bump of trees and you decide to sit on one of the big shiny rock.
It has a few little dents in it.
It has iridescent colors in it.
Blue, pinks and purples.
You think this is a pretty rock.
It feels very smooth and it's rather shiny for a rock.
You sit yourself down and you think it's nice and warm.
Is it moving?
Oh don't be silly. Of course it's not moving.
Then you hear a voice "Get off my back!"
You jump off the rock and think who said that.
You look down as this rock really does move this time.
A little head pops out with an orange hat.

You are absolutely flabbergasted!
Is this rock alive?
Hmm well actually no, it's not a rock.
It's actually a huge turtle
This turtle with the orange hat is looking directly at you.
You say "Oh I'm really sorry! I didn't mean to sit on you. I thought you were a rock!"
The turtle laughs and says, "Okay I'll let you off."
It's a female turtle.
She looks and says, "My name is Tessie. What's yours?"
So, you tell her your name.

You ask her why she's just sitting there just doing nothing.
She tells you with a little sad look on her face, "Well do you see these vines on this tree?"
You say, "Hmm yea, I didn't notice it before but yeah."
"Well I've got one of the feet stuck in it and I can't get out. I've tried to bit it but it won't come off."
"Oh dear," you say, "well I can help."
So you kneel down in the warm sand and you dig a little bit because a foot has gone into the sun completely.

You see that the vine has wrapped itself around her lovely little foot.

She really can't move.

Very gently you lift her foot and you unwrap the wine from it.

You actually look at her foot and she's got little tiny nails.

They're painted orange.

She has orange toenails just like her hat.

You smile to yourself because you think it looks rather pretty.

You untangle Tessie completely and she stretches her leg.

She says, "Oh that feels so much better. I can move again! Thank you so much for being so kind to me, even though you did sit on me."

You laugh a little and you think oh she's really nice.

Tessie looks as you and says, "Would you like to ride on my back? I'm big and strong because I really am a big turtle."

You say yes.

"Please come on," she says.

So, you climb on her back and she lifts herself up to a full height.

She really is quite bit.

She slowly starts moving because she can't go very fast.

After all she is a turtle.

You wobble a bit but you keep ahold of her shell.
It wobbles from side to side as she lumbers along the sand.
It's amazing this beautiful creature is letting you ride on her back.
Or is it because you were so kind to her?
You feel good because you are kind to her.
You know that it's always good to be kind.
Always.

Tessie the turtle reaches the water.
She starts to walk in it and it gets deeper.
You feel your feet dangling in the water.
She turns to you and she says, "Would you like to go for a swim with me? I'll keep you safe. I'll keep you safe on my back as long as you keep a tight hold."
You think yeah why not. I can do that.
So, Tessie moves further and deeper into the water.
Then she begins to swim and it is amazing.
You are sitting on the back of a turtle in the biggest and deepest blue ocean you've ever seen.
It's not as wobbly now because she's not lumbering on the beach.
It's like you are floating because you can't see her legs which are swimming really quickly underneath you, but you can't see that.
It's like you're floating on a giant rock.

A giant rock with a head with an orange hat.
The sun is shining and it is so lovely and warm.
As Tessie head further out, it is so beautiful.
So so beautiful.
The waves are gentle.

As she swims further out you look around.
You can see a very large ship in the distance.
So far away it looks tiny, but you know it's a really big ship.
You turn to look somewhere else and there's a smaller ship.
Or maybe it's just because it's even further away?
You don't really know.
Tessie keeps swimming and as she does, she begins to chat.
She tells you she is 104 years old.
Oh my goodness!
Does anyone ever live to be 104 years old?
You turn to look behind you and as you do, you realize you are very very far out at sea.
The shore that you were on, the lovely golden white beach, is so tiny now.
You're not afraid.
You're really enjoying this and you know Tessie will keep you safe.

You turn back as Tessie chatters away telling you about her life, about her family, how many children she's got.
Lots and lots of children.
You look ahead of you again and you see a whale.
This huge enormous whale.
You see its tail come out of the water and go back down with a big splash.
You think oh that's a bit big.
Oh maybe we shouldn't get to close to it.
Tessie says, "Its okay. That's my friend Bert the whale."
Such an odd name for a whale.
She swims closer and right up to Bert.
Bert's eye is probably about the size of my head!
You think wow Bert can talk too!
He says, "Hello Tessie. What are you doing today? Where are you going? Who's that on your back?"
"This is my friend who helped me by untangling my foot, so im giving this beautiful little human a ride on my back."

You really are a kind person.
Okay Tessie. I'm off. I've got things to do today.
With a great big splash she dives into the water and you get drenched, but you laugh.

You don't fall off Tessie's back.
The water goes everywhere.
You can even taste it.
It's salty.
You and Tessie just laugh and then Tessie asks, "Would you like to see to where I live."
Well yes, but do you live on the beach?
Tessie says, "Now I live beneath the water."
I can't do that!
She says, "Yes you can."
With a quick flip of one of her feet, she throws a kind of mask on you.
You have no idea where she got it from but she gives it to you.
"You should put that on your face and you'll be absolutely fine. You'll be able to breath no problem at all."
What that she dives completely under the water.
You barely have time to get your mask on.

As you look around you are amazing.
You are beneath the ocean and actually bright and lit down here.
There are fish swimming past.
Lots and lots of fish.
They all nod to Tessie as they go past.

All different colors and different varieties.
Striped ones, spotty ones, beautiful bright blue ones.
You have no idea what they're called.
Tessie continues to swim.
She goes down and down and down.
She does not do too deep though.
What you see coming towards you is a lot of coral.
Behind that coral is brightly colored coral.
It looks like a little cave.
Tessie takes you into that cave.
When you get inside, the cave it lit up with sparkling lights.
Sparkling shining crystals.
There are other turtles in there.
Lots of them in fact.

Tessie said, "This is my family and all these turtles are my children."
There are hundreds of them.
This is a very large cave.
For a few moments you can swim around with Tessie and meet Tessie's children.
You find out what they do.
You find out if they all live together or do they have their own caves?

Ask them.

Maybe when you've met all of Tessie's children you could see if there are other caves.

There are lots of other caves and maybe you could swim around the ocean with Tessie, meet her friends, meet other sea creatures.

Maybe you can find birds and that whale again.

You can do anything you like here.

You can do it all with Tessie.

She will show you exactly where she lives.

If you like you could call it a village.

Not a village as you know it but it's her village.

It's her town.

It's her city.

You can do anything you want.

You might even find out that maybe they've got a fun fair too.

Oh would that be nice?

Maybe you could have an ice cream cone.

You imagine having ice cream underwater.

Now it's time for Tessie to take you back.

You had a wonderful time meeting her family and her friends.

You make sure you're back on Tessie's back.

She begins to swim very quickly and in no time at all your back.

Tessie has arrived back on the sandy shore.
You climb off her back.
You wonder what you're going to do now.
You're feeling a bit sleepy now.
You had a very exciting day so Tessie says, "Tell you what. Let you and I have a little sleep under this clump of trees. If I snuggle down, you can lean up against me and pretend I'm your pillow."
You think to yourself that is a really good idea because your eyes are beginning to close.
You get more tired by the second.
Tessie lays herself down, tucks in her feet and all you can see is part of her little hat.
Her bright orange hat sticking out.
You stretch beside her and lay on your back.
On her enormous shell is actually quite comfortable.
You put your head back and close your eyes.
Tessie says, "Wow. What a lovely day we had together. I really enjoyed meeting you. I want to regard you as a my very very special friend. You've been so kind to me. You know if you ever come back here again, we can always go and visit my family and my friends."
You mumble to yourself that would be nice.
You're so sleepy now so so tired.
You know that when you wake up, you will be back in your very own bed.

In your very own little room with the most wonderful memories of Tessie, the very large turtle.
So now just sleep.
Just rest.
Goodnight.
Sleep tight.

Now imagine you are walking towards the ocean.
Walking through a beautiful tropical forest.
You can see the trees around you.
Very tall and elegant trees.
You can smell the fresh clean air.
You can even hear the sounds of all the different animals and birds in this forest.
Can you hear them?

You can hear the waves up ahead of you.
You can hear the sounds of them coming up.
You can even smell the ocean spray.
That lovely smell you can only find at the beach.
Can you smell it?
You continue to walk along your path coming close to the sea.
As you come to the edge of the trees you see a brilliant blue color of ocean ahead.

You can hear the magnificent sound of the ocean waves, so much louder now.
You walk out of the forest and onto a long stretch of glorious white sand.
The sun is very soft, so you take off your shoes and socks.
You walk through the hot white sand towards the water.
You can feel the sun beneath your feet.
Feel it between your toes.
Can you feel it?
The beach is very wide and very long.
It stretches for miles ahead.
You can hear the waves going into the shore.
You can smell the clean salt water.
You can even smell the sand.
You look again at the ocean and it's the deepest blue that you have ever seen.
Now imagine yourself walking towards the water over the fine hot sand.
You're feeling a bit hot and just a little sticky now too.
As you walk you can see the sparkles of the sunshine dance upon the water's surface like a million tiny stars all shining just for you.
It looks so beautiful.

A wave washes over the sun towards you.
You can feel it touch your toes before gently receding.
You step forwards and more waves wash over your feet.
It feels so cool and refreshing.
So calming on your feet.
You walk a bit further into the clear clean water.
You can see the white sand under the water.
You can feel it between your toes.
Can you feel it?
Squash your toes into the sand.

Wiggle them about in the water.
You can see a few small fish rapidly swim past you.
Flashes of color as they pass by.
The water is very pleasant.
Cool but not too cold.

You walk a bit further into the water.
You decide you want to take a gentle swim.

Just enjoy the ocean for a few minutes.
Allow yourself to float and drift around in the beautiful deep blue ocean.

Just float around with all the little fish and just relax.

Now you are feeling very calm and refreshed.
You're feeling very peaceful and very very relaxed.
You walk out of the water and back onto the beach.
Feeling again the soft sand beneath your feet and your toes.
You walk along the water's edge and you feel free of any worries you might have had.
They've all gone.
All of your problems have been washed away.
You only feel very calm and very peaceful and so so relaxed.

You turn around and see a comfortable lounge chair and towel just for you.

You go over and you sit or lie there on the chair.
You may decide to spread the towel in the sun and just relax on the chair.
Just relaxing and enjoying the sunshine.
Enjoying the cool gentle breeze upon your face.
The warmth of the sun on your skin.
The sounds of the waves making you feel ever so peaceful and ever so happy.

You just watch the waves as they ebb and flow backwards and forwards.
Backwards and forwards.
You feel calm.
So calm.
So relaxed and so very very peaceful.
You just sit there either for a little while longer.
Enjoying this lovely relaxation that's been made just for you.

Now it's time for you to return back to your normal life.
It's time to come back home.
Now imagine you're walking on the most glorious sandy beach.
It's very soft and very white.

You can hear the gentle sound of the waves as the roll on the sandy beach.
You can even smell the ocean spray.
That lovely smell you can only find at the beach.
The ocean is a brilliant deep blue color.
The sounds of the ocean waves is so much louder now.
You walk through the hot white sand towards the water.

You can feel the sand beneath your feet.
You can feel it between your toes.

The beach is very long and it stretches for miles ahead.
You go over and you step into the water and it covers your ankles.
It feels so cool and fresh on your skin.
There are large rocks and what seems to look like a cave further along the beach.
You think to yourself that maybe you'll explore it later.
For now you just keep paddling along.
You notice something in the ocean near those rocks.
You spot the head of a seal bobbing up and own.
It seems to be very near the cave you just noticed.
You decide to go over and take a look.
What you see is a tiny white seal.
It looks like it may be struggling.
You wonder what's wrong.
The tiny white seal looks like it's caught in something.

You call out to the little seal and you ask if it's okay.
A tiny little voice shouts, "Please help me!"

You rush over and you see that the little seal is caught in an old fishing line.
It's tangled around its flippers, so you go straight over and help that little seal break free.
The little seal gives you a great big grin.
"Thank you very much for your help."
The little seal tells you his name.
His name is heart.
Heart is a very tiny white seal.
He's so tiny he could fit into the palm of your hand.
He has the biggest blue eyes you have ever seen.
They are so bright and so kind.
Heart tells you that he loves going on adventures.
He loves going to swim lessons and on boat rides with his family.
He loves exploring places he's never been before.
Although, sometimes it gets him into trouble.
You see, his parents worry about him very much when he doesn't tell them where he's going, or even who he is with because they always go places together as a family.
They never go anywhere without each other.

Sometimes heart gets so excited about where he wants to go he forgets to tell them.
He just swims off.

Heart is the baby of the family so he really shouldn't be going anywhere on his own just yet.

Just now you hear voices calling.

It sounds like they're coming from the cave you wanted to explore, so you and Heart swim over there and take a look.

Heart recognizes the voices and it's his family.

It's his mom, his dad and his auntie.

They have been looking everywhere for Heart.

They swim over to you both with big smiles on their faces.

They are so relieved to have found Heart and that he's okay.

They have been worried sick looking for him.

They all chatter at once.

You can't really understand what they're saying.

They're all talking together but they are happy.

Heart introduces you to his family.

The biggest seal comes up to you and Heart says this is my dad Blobby.

Blobby is the biggest out of the family.

He has a beautiful gray color with majestic black.

Blobby is a super chunky seal and very round.

Next Heart introduces you to his mom.

Her name is Sweetie and she is smaller than Blobby.

She is a very beautiful white seal with lovely soft fluffy fur.

She has the sweetest black eyes and Heart looks very like his mom.

Finally Heart introduces you to his aunt.
Her name is Spot.
Spot is a spotted grey seal with kind and very wise yellow eyes.
She is the longest seal out of all of them.
Spot is Blobby's sister.
Heart tells them how you rescued him and how you untangled him from the net.
They can't thank you enough.
They are so happy.
As a reward they invite you to tour their house.
Blobby says, "Get on my back. It'll be much quicker."

You climb up on Blobby's back.
It's so comfortable and so soft, but you hang on tight.
Blobby says, "Okay we are all ready to go!"
Within seconds you are going at a great speed.
It's fantastic!
Water is splashing everywhere, and you absolutely love it.
The five of you ride off to Heart's home.

You enjoy the ride.

You arrive at their home and you are amazed.
It's actually a boat.
You thought that all seals lived under the ocean waves.
Well this family lives on an actual boat!

They live on a boat that bobs up and down in the sea.
How cool is that?
This isn't just any old boat though, this boat is shaped like a seal.
It is huge!
It even has a flag flying high on the top of the mast with a picture of a seal on it too.
It's very luxurious.
Wow! You have never seen anything like this before.
It's wonderful!
Sweetie goes into the kitchen saying that she's going to make a pot of tea now for the adults.
But for you and Heart there's freshly squeezed orange juice.
While you wait for Sweetie to make the tea, you have a little look around the room you are in.
There are family photos everywhere.

There is a bookcase overcrowded with books of all kinds.
They obviously all like to read here.
You even see one of your favorite stories on one of the shelves.
There is a really big log fire burning.
There are big squishy comfy chairs all around and even bigger squishier sofas.
There are lovely vases filled with flowers of all sorts of colors.
There even is a tropical fish tank full of brightly colored fish.
Heart says that they are his pets.
He loves fishes and they are his friends.
You feels so comfy and so warm here.
You think it would be great if you could live on a boat like this.
Heart asks you is you would like to see the rest of the boat.
He says he will show you his bedroom too.
You set off and have a good explore around his lovely home.
For a few moments you see what else there is to find.
How many rooms are there on this very big boat that looks like a seal?

Just have fun with Heart for a few moments while you wait for your tea.

You and Heart now return to the lovely comfy living room and meet up with Blobby, Sweetie and Spot.
They are all sitting around a small table with your drinks on it and the biggest and fattest chocolate cake you have ever seen.
Wow! That's a lot of chocolate!
Heart tells you that his mom made it.
She makes the best cakes in the whole wide world.
You take a bit out of your piece of the cake and wholeheartedly agree with him.
It is delicious and very chocolaty.
The five of you happily eat your chocolate cake and drink your drinks.

Heart gives you a great big yawn.
Then you do too.
Sweetie asks you if you would like a sleepover with Heart.
You say you can stay in his room with him and say "Oh yes please. That would be lovely."
Blobby and Spot say goodnight to both of you and Sweetie takes you and Heart ot his bedroom.
She tucks you both and says goodnight.

Then she switches off the lights.
It's then that an amazing thing happens.
There's a big round window in the ceiling of Heart's bedroom that you didn't notice before.
Through this window you can see the moon high up in the sky.
You can see lots and lots of stars all gently shining down on your beds.
It's like you have your own private show of dancing lights.
It's so beautiful.
You both watched the stars feeling so peaceful, so calm and so happy.
You begin to feel your eyes getting very heavy and a bit sleepy.

You can hear the gentle lapping of the waves, as they move against the side of the boat.
This makes you feel so safe.
You feel your eyes gently closing now as you take a deep breath in and let out a long happy sigh.
You have made a very special friend today who has a very special family too.
Remember you can come visit heart and his family anytime you want to.
You can visit Blobby, Sweetie and Spot too.

You take another deep breath in and slowly breathe out.

Feeling that your body has already gone to sleep, you gently close your eyes and drift into the most wonderful sleep.

Always remember you are safe.

You are loved and you are protected.

Always.

CHAPTER 4

Magical Forest Friends

Close your eyes and be very still.
Take a big deep breath in through your nose, and slowly and gently breathe out through your mouth.
Take another deep breath in and slowly and gently breathe out through your mouth.
One more time, big deep breathe in and slowly and gently breath out through your mouth.
Relax feeling peaceful and calm.
Now, imagine that you are surrounded by a beautiful white light.
This light surrounds your whole body and it's beneath your feet and above your head.
You are inside this light just like a caterpillar safe in its cocoon.

This light is very special and inside this light you know that you are always safe.
You know that you are always loved.
You know that you are always protected.

Now, imagine that you are outdoors walking in a lovely green forest.
The nighttime is approaching fast, but at the moment it's still light out.
The sun is beginning to set and the sky is starting to darken ever so slightly.
The air around you is still and calm.
You can hear all the different sounds as the creatures of the forest begin to settle for the night.
Can you hear them?
The birds are flying home to rest now.
The tiny animals are rushing to their homes.
Can you see the foxes calling out to each other as they come out for the night to begin their hunt, or food, or just to play with each and have some fun.
Can you hear the sounds of breaking twigs and the rustle of leaves as each tiny animal scurries to their warm safe home.
As you walk along, you hear a different sound coming from the treetops high above.
You're not sure what it is yet.

You listen harder and you realize that what you are hearing is the call of the night owl.

The sound of a very large owl indeed.

You walk a bit deeper into the lush forest as the sky gets darker still.

It feels so peaceful here, so calming and the night is quieter.

There are now no sounds of any animals as they are all tucked into their warm cuzy homes.

The birds are all asleep in their nests, but you hear the call of the night owl.

You hear the flapping of its large but gentle wings.

The sound gets closer to you when suddenly right before you plops down with big round glasses perched on the end of his nose.

Startled, you take a step back wondering what to do.

The large owl nods his head at you and says, "Good evening."

He pushes his glasses back upon his nose because they keep sliding down.

Your mouth drops open and you think to yourself did this owl just speak to me?

Well yes, he did.

Because you didn't answer the old owl clears his throat again with a big hmm and says again, "good evening."

You say it back to him with a smile.

The owl smiles back and tells you he is off for a fly around.
He says he spotted you from high above, when he thought to himself if you would like to fly with me.
So he flew down to ask you.
He often asks little humans if they would like to fly with him.
He says that he gets rather lonely flying on his own.
You are so excited by this that you say, "Oh yes please! Who wouldn't want to fly with an owl. I know I would!"
As you look around you notice that the sun has gone down and been replaced by a beautiful silver moon.
It's actually quite dark now.
You can see all around you with the shining glow of the moonlight.
The old owl who is very larger than you tells you to grab hold of his feathers and pull yourself up onto hit back.
He tells you not to pull any of his feathers out though as it will hurt a lot.
You grab the old owl's feathers and heave yourself up onto his back being very careful.
He then tells you to hold on tight.
He begins to run flapping his huge wings.
The old owl runs and runs and runs but nothing seems to be happening.

Nothing seems to be happening, but the old owl still keeps running.

He's now starting to get a bit puffed and his huge wings keep flapping away.

You look ahead and you see that you are heading towards the edge of a cliff.

Oh no!

You're starting to get a bit worried now, as the cliff edge is getting very close.

The old owl hasn't even taken off yet but the old owl still keeps running.

He is still puffing away.

Then just as you get to the edge of the cliff the old owl jumps off.

Then the two of you swoop down going faster and faster.

The old owls wings are spread really wide and flapping away like crazy.

You close your eyes really tight and cling onto the owl's feathers.

Just as you think you're going to crash the old owl lifts himself higher and higher up into the night sky.

You slowly open your eyes and take a look around.

What you see takes your breath away.

You are high up in the sky gliding on the back of the owl.

The moon is shining brightly and the stars are twinkling like beautiful diamonds in the sky.

It's so still and quiet up here.
All you can hear is the gentle breeze as it washes over you.
The old owl is no longer flapping his wings.
He is gliding on the currents of air all around you.
He turns his body to the left and you look below you.
Far below you is a beautiful lake surrounded by your lovely forest.
You can see the reflection of the moon on the water's surface.
You can even see your own reflection on the back of the owl as he gets closer to the water.
For a few more moments you fly with this beautiful old owl.
You feel the gentle breeze on your face.
Talk to the owl and ask what his name.
You can ask him whatever you want.
Don't forget to tell him who you are as well.
For now just fly.

The beautiful old owl returns you to the ground of your forest.
You gently land and thank this beautiful creature for letting you fly with him.
You ask if it would be possible for you to do this again.
He says of course it is.

All you have to do is go for an evening walk in the forest look and he will be there.

The old owl flaps his huge wings, runs for a little bit and then takes off.

You watch him disappear up into the night sky.

You can hear him make the sound that only owls can make, as he slowly gets smaller and smaller.

You feel so happy and so content now.

So peaceful.

Now it's time to leave this beautiful place, leave the beautiful wise old owl.

You can come and visit him anytime you want.

Now you are back in your own bed.

As you gently rest take a deep breath and slowly breathe out.

Feel yourself becoming more and more relaxed.

One more time deep breath and gently breathe out more and more sleepy.

So peaceful.

Now, imagine that you are in a very lush green forest and the sun is shining.

It's a very beautiful day.

The sun is peeking through the leaves and the branches of the tall trees.

There are so many trees.

You feel very calm, very relaxed and very very peaceful.

You can hear birds singing to each other.

Can you hear them flying from tree to tree to have a little char with each other?
They sound so happy as they tweet away high up in the branches.
Can you hear the birds singing?
Can you hear them chatting to each other?
As you walk along you notice something ahead of you sitting against a very tall and bushy tree.
You are not sure what it is so you walk a bit quicker.
As you look and get closer to the tree, you realize it's a fox!
It's a rather beautiful fox with a very bushy red tail pointing straight up.
This fox is sitting cross legged at the base of the tree with his eyes closed.
He looks like he's meditating and you can hear the beautiful sound of the Tibetan singing bowl but you can not see one anywhere.

You can even smell incense burning a lovely sweet aroma.
It kind of tickles your nostrils.
You don't want to disturb the fox so you stop and stand still.
You just watch and notice that he has on very brightly colored trousers with lots of red, blues and even purple colors.

He is also wearing a very shiny silver waistcoat with really bright yellow buttons.

He looks like he's got tiny suns all over him.

He also has the biggest orange hat you have ever seen with a big pink feather sticking out form the top.

He is a colorful sight to see.

It's like he had no idea what to wear when he got dresses this morning so he put all of his cloths on.

He also has a very large metal framed glasses on.

Normally foxes are very shy and try to hide themselves away but this one clearly isn't.

As you stand there trying to be ever so quiet he opens his eyes and peers over the top of his glasses.

He gives you a great big smile and says, "Hello. How can I help you today?"

You tell him you were just out walking and came across him but did not want to disturb him so tried to be very quiet.

He smiles again and tells you to come and sit beside him so you do.

He tells you his name is Mr. Chi and he asks what your name is so you tell him.

Around Mr. Chi's neck is a mala bead necklace.

They are beads that help you when you meditate.

They are very beautiful.

Mr. Chi pulls another set of mala beads out of his pick and gives them to you as a gift.

He tells you to put them on.
You thank him for his lovely gift and you put on the necklace.
He asks if you would like to meditate with him and you say, "Oh yes! I'd like to do that!"
All he wants you to do is close your eyes and just breathe gently in and out, in and out.
So you do as he asks.

With your eyes closed you can hear the sound of the Tibetan singing bowl even more clearly now but you still can't see it.
You can smell the incense even stronger.
Can you smell it?
Can you smell how strong it is?
You realize that you can hear Mr. Chi speaking but he's not using his voice to speak you can hear his thoughts in your mind.
How clever Mr. Chi is with his voice.
In your mind he asks you again how can he help you so you sit and think for a moment and then you tell him.
You tell him whatever is on your mind and whatever may be worrying you.
So, for a few moments you just sit with Mr. Chi and tell him what is on your mind and he will give you

the answer that you need to hear because Mr. Chi has all the answers to everything.

Mr. Chi can solve any problem because Mr. Chi is a very clever fox.

Mr. Chi now asks you to open your eyes and just breathe gently and slowly for a minute or so.

He asks you to come with him into his den for a nice cool drink and a biscuit so that you can have a chat.

You both get up and walk around to the back of the tree where there is a door which Mr. Chi opens and you both enter the lovely room.

The room is very comfortable and very colorful just like Mr. Chi.

There are beads hanging everywhere.

There are beads on the walls.

There are beads hanging over his cozy little lamps.

There are even beads hanging from the ceiling all in many different colors.

There is a nice warm flower glowing and there are flowers everywhere.

Mr. Chi likes flowers.

He tells you his favorite flowers are tulips and he asks you what your favorite flower is and you tell him.

Mr. Chi tells you to sit in his best chair which is a nice big concrete armchair with lots of colorful cushions on it.
There is color everywhere in Mr. Chi's home.

You sit down on his best chair and take the cool drink Mr. Chi offers you.
Beside the comfy chair is a little table and Mr. Chi puts down on it a plate of delicious biscuits.
For a few moments you just sit with Mr. Chi, the clever fox, and have a chat about anything you want.
Maybe you can ask Mr. Chi how is he cleverest fox in the kingdom.
You can ask him why everyone comes to him with their problems.
Maybe you can even ask him where on Earth did he get those crazy cloths from.
This is now your time with the clever fox so make the most of it as he a busy fox.
Whatever you feel like talking about Mr Chi will listen because today you are his favorite person.

Now it's time for you to say goodbye to Mr. Chi and thank him for letting you meditate and chat with him and for seeing those amazing clothes.

It's time for you to thank him for giving you a lovely cool drink and some of your favorite biscuits.

It's time for you to leave his lovely cozy den and to return to your lovely home.

Now, imagine that you are in a beautiful lush green jungle and this jungle has the most amazing trees.

Some of them are very tall.

So tall that they look as if they are almost touching the sky.

Some of them are a bit smaller and a bit fatter.

Some of them have very strange vines dangling from them.

You are deep in the jungle and you realize that you've been hearing lots of strange noises.

You're not really sure where they are coming from, but they don't scare you at all.

You can hear the sounds of birds as they fly from treetop to treetop.

There are several different birds calling out to each other and you can hear them.

You can also hear the breeze fluttering through the leaves on the tree tops.

Stop just for a second and close your eyes.

Enjoy the variety of all the different sounds all around you.

You can hear the sounds of a big jungle cat far off in the distance and you can hear him calling out to his family.
Maybe he's calling them home for supper.
Maybe he just wants to know where they are.
You can even hear the sound of monkeys chattering to each other.
Can you hear them?
Some of them are quite loud.
You wonder what they are saying to each other.

If you listen really hard, you might be able to understand what they are saying.
Take a moment and listen to them.

You continue to walk through this lovely lush green jungle but you've never noticed before just how many shades of green there are.
Its beautiful.
The light in the forest cascades down through the leaves like twinkling lights.
There are plants and moss everywhere.
You can hear the many tiny animals of the jungle all moving out of the way running fast hoping you can't see them.
They are too quick for you.

You notice that the sun is starting to dip.
There is a lovely orange red glow in the sky.
You can see the colors of the sky peeking through the top of the trees.
As you continue your walk you come across an old fallen tree just lying on the ground.
You decide to have a little sit and rest your legs.
As you sit there, you can hear movement behind you.
You turn to have a look your mouth drops open in a gasp.
You are amazed because standing in front of you is a chimpanzee.
A chimpanzee with a bright red bowtie around his neck and a bright red hat sitting on top of his head.
The chimpanzee tips his hat to you and says good afternoon.
Did this chimpanzee really just say good afternoon?
Before you can reply, he sits himself down next to you and makes himself comfortable.
He takes off his hat and lays it gently on the fallen tree.
He gives you a very big grin.
He tells you that his is gathering friends for his afternoon tea.
He asks if you would like to come too.
You would love to come and how lovely would that be.

The chimpanzee puts his red hat back on and stands up.
He says, "Okay then follow me!"
The two of you set off together.
You go off and gather the rest of the chimpanzee's friends.
After a little while, you come across a very big tiger with a very large head.
He is also wearing a bow tie but blue.
He also has a big cowboy hat.
He grins at you and you notice he has very large teeth.
He is not scary at all, in fact, he is a bid old softie.
The three of you keep on moving.
You keep on moving along just looking around.
You come across to a clearing of the jungle.
In the middle of the clearing there is a table and five chairs.
Sitting at the table is a very large elephant with a with bow tie around his neck and a large floppy white hat.
Next to him is a snake who also has a pink bow tie to match hit pink hat.
The chimpanzee and the tiger walk over and sit down.
The beckon you to sit down on the remaining chair.
You look down at the table and see a big flowery teapot with five China cups and saucers.

There is a sugar bowl and fresh cup of milk.

There are scones with strawberry jam and fresh whipped cream.

There is a huge plate of cookies of various sizes and shapes.

There is also a large chocolate cake sitting in the center of the table with flakes of chocolate all around it.

There is also a plate of peanut butter sandwiches for everyone.

There is a massive pitcher filled with lemonade for anyone who would not want to drink tea.

There is a bowl filled to the top of fresh apples, bananas, pears, oranges, peaches and many other different kinds of fruits.

It is like a big feast!

Everything looks so delicious and a good thing you're hungry!

The chimpanzee realizes that no one has told you their names.

So, he introduces himself and his friends.

He tells you that his name is Chico Chico the chimpanzee, his friends are Tommy the tiger, Eddie the elephant and Sid the snake.

He asks you what your name is so you tell him.

You ask them why they are all wearing bowties and hats.
Sid says because they always get dressed up for afternoon tea.
It wouldn't be proper if they didn't.
For a little while you just sit with your new friends and enjoy your feast.
Ask them all the questions that are bouncing around in your head.
Ask them where they all live, who they live with and anything else you want to ask.
They are so thrilled that you are having afternoon tea with them.
They say they don't have important guests very often.
Now, is your chance to ask all the things you wanted to about the lives of chimpanzees, tigers, elephants and snakes.

Now, it's time for the tea party to end.
Everyone has to go home now, and you have to go home too.
So, you stand up and thank these beautiful animals for inviting you to their Tea Party.
Thank them all for the lovely food, but most of all thank them for telling you all about their lives in this huge lush green jungle.

Chico the chimpanzee hands you a little box with a silver ribbon tied around it.
He tells you that it is a gift for you.
You thank him very much for the wonderful gift.
He tells you that if you ever want to come to the tea party again all you have to do is come to the lush green jungle and he will find you.
You smile and you wave goodbye to your new friends and start to walk away.

Now, imagine that you are in a beautiful lush green rainforest.
This forest has the most amazing trees and some of them are very tall indeed.
So tall in fact that they look as if they are touching the sky.
There are so many luscious green trees here.
You can hear all kinds of sounds coming from the forest.
You can hear lots of different birds.
You can hear the sounds of animals moving around.
You can even hear sounds of water running over rocks.
You can't see it, but you can hear it.
It is very relaxing.
You find yourself walking along a path that winds in and out on the forest floor.

You are just enjoying yourself in this beautiful rainforest minding your own business when suddenly you hear the sounds of snoring, loud thunderous snoring.

My goodness!

You follow the sound until it leads you to a tree that looks very interesting.

You step in front of it and take a good look where the snoring is coming from.

The snoring is so loud now that you have to cover your ears.

You are wondering what on earth is making that sound.

They must be very deep asleep.

This particular tree looks like a secret tree house.

There is a sign carved into the tree saying, "Berry Norma Residence."

You wonder what on earth is Berry and Norman.

The snoring suddenly stops, and you hear movement coming from above.

You look upwards trying to see what is moving around up there.

Your eyes adjust and then to your surprise you see a sloth!

Its tail is wound around the branches and is hanging upside down looking at you with very big sleepy eyes.

They move extremely slowly, and they love being high up in the treetops.

To your surprise the sloth speaks to you and says, "Hello!"

It's a girl sloth and tells you her name is Amazing.

Amazing has a bright yellow hat with a big green feather in it.

It makes her look as if sunshine is coming out from the top of her head.

You say hello back to Amazing and you tell her your name.

She asks if you would like to come up and meet her family and see where she lives.

You say, "Of course!"

Amazing drops down a rope ladder for you and you climb up.

You would love to live high up in the treetops like her.

When you reach the first level there is a spiral staircase and it's wrapped around the whole tree.

When you get to the top of the staircase you stand next to amazing.

She adjusts her big yellow hat and says, "Follow me."

Amazing takes you to her front door and you see that her house is a wooden circular lodge.

Her home is made purely for snooze, relaxation and sleep.

There are big soft fluffy cushions everywhere.

There is also a speaker system playing sweet relaxation music.

You really like Amazing's home.

Amazing introduces you to her dad Barry.

You notice he has an earring on his left ear and a baseball cap on his head.

Her mom is called Norma and he only has one slipper one because she doesn't know where the other one is.

Cyril is her brother who is Amazing's older brother.

He is a grumpy teenager who keeps picking his nose.

Amazing seems to be the only normal one in her family.

This family has the best music and they love playing it very loudly.

You take a walk over to the window and take a look outside.

You can see the beautiful panoramic view above the treetops of the rainforest.

You notice this lovely family of sloths have a speaker system scattered all around the forest.

When you turn around everything is like in slow motion.

They even speak in slow motion.

Norma gives you a nice cup of tea and you all sit down and have a little chat.

You tell them all about your family, where you live, what your favorite things are and who your best friend is.

For a few moments sit and chat with this amazing family of sloths.

Find out about them too and don't forget to drink your cup of tea!

When you finished your tea, Barry says, "its now time for sleep."

He asks you if you would like to stay and have a little nap too.

Of course you say yes!

They have been up for two already and they are exhausted.

It's nice to have a chat with new friends.

Sloths like to get at least 18 hours of sleep because their world is so very slow.

You realize that outside of this amazing home, there is light rain falling.

It's making you feel very sleep listening to it.

You go outside and you choose a very comfy chair.

It's a comfy chair indeed.

It has a big soft pillow for your head.

You take a seat and you can hear the soft gentle music playing through their amazing speaker system.

It's making you feel very drowsy.

It makes you feel so sleepy.

So sleepy that you finally find it hard to open your eyes.

That's okay because you don't have to open your eyes if you don't want to.

All you have to do is relax.

You're in the chair with a big soft pillow listening to the rain as it helps you to fall gently to sleep.

Can you hear the soft and wonderful sounds of the beautiful music?

You are drifting deeper and deeper into the most wonderful night's sleep ever.

So snuggle down.

You feel so safe and so protected.

So very loved.

When you wake up in the morning you will feel completely refreshed, bright, alert and ready to begin the new amazing day ahead.

Each night from now on, you will sleep better and better.

Deeper and deeper.

Night night.

Sleep tight.

CHAPTER 5

Positive Bedtime Affirmations

Welcome to your happiness and imagination affirmations.

This is where we will focus only of the good feelings when we talk to ourselves in a positive way.

We feel good and great when amazing things happen in our lives.

Listen to these positive affirmations and repeat them in your head or out loud.

Great things flow to me.

I am a great listener.

People listen to me.

I am blessed.

The world needs me.

I have a brilliant brain.

I am growing up to be happy and healthy.

Everything always goes well for me.
I am generous.
I am helpful.
I am kind to others, and I am kind to myself.
I have so many people that love me.
Sharing is caring.
I can use my imagination to create great things.
I sleep deeply every night.
I believe I am great.
I tell the truth.
I speak kind words.
I share my feelings.
My feelings are important.
I make good choices.
I feel warm and fuzzy on the inside.
Healthy food makes my body feel good.
I stand up tall and I sit up straight.
I am proud of who I am.
I am full of amazing ideas.
I feel grateful for all the fun things and people in the world.
I love our beautiful planet Earth.
I love the trees, the clouds, the Sun and the breeze.
The trees, birds, and animals are my friends.
I love all of the wonderful animals on Earth.
I love sharing our planet with so many interesting people.

I sleep deeply every night like I'm on a fluffy cloud.
I can make my dreams come true.
I can choose to feel happy at any time.
I am free.
I am made of stardust.
I am a star.
I shine bright every day.
When I ask for help, I always get the help I need.
I have a super day every day.
I respect others and others respect me.
It feels good to use my manners.
When other people make mistakes I forgive them quickly.
When I make mistakes I forgive myself quickly.
Just like the clouds clear when it stops raining, bad times don't last forever. The Sun always shines brighter.
I feel calm and peaceful.
I can be whatever I want to be.
I love dreaming big with my imagination.
I love my body, my hair, my skin, my eyes and my nose.
I am perfect as I am.
I love being me.
Smiling makes me feel happy.
I am always super healthy.
I have everything I need.

I am always safe.
I always do my best.
I believe in myself.
I am loved.
I am smart.
I feel so happy like it's my birthday every day.
I am brave.
I can do anything.
I think positive thoughts.
My mind is powerful.
I sleep deeply every night.
I am so kind to others and I am kind to myself.
I have so many people that love me.
I love my friends and my friends love me.
I can create anything.
I am a creative genius.
I am the painter of my life.
What I feel is important.
I love having fun.
There is always more fun ahead.
I say thank you for all the wonderful things in my life.
Thank you.
Thank you.
Thank you.
I say thank you for all the exciting things in my future.
Thank you.

Thank you.
Thank you.
I am perfect as I am.
I'm a supper happy super kid.
I play well with others.
I am very special.
I am unique.
There is only one of me in the whole world.
I have so much exciting energy.
I love learning new things.
I'm a fast learner.
I am more than enough just as I am.
I am important.
I am worth of all great things.
I deserve all great things.
I sleep deeply every night.
Great things flow to me.
I'm a great listener.
People listen to me.
I am blessed.
The world needs me.
I have a brilliant brain.
I am growing up to be happy and healthy.
Everything always goes so well for me.
I am generous.
I am helpful.
I am kind to others and I am kind to myself.

I have so many people that love me.
Sharing is caring.
I can use my imagination to create great things.
I sleep deeply every night.
I believe I am great.
I tell the truth.
I speak kind words.
I make good choices.
I feel warm and fuzzy on the inside.
Healthy food makes my body feel good.
I stand up tall and I sit up straight.
I am proud of who I am.
I am full of amazing ideas.
I feel grateful for all the fun things and people in the world.
I love our beautiful planet Earth.
I love the trees, the clouds, the sun and the breeze.
The trees, birds and animals are my friends.
I love all the wonderful animals on Earth.
I love sharing our planet with so many interesting people.
I sleep deeply every night like I'm on a fluffy cloud.
I can make my dreams come true.
I can choose to be happy at any time.
I am free.
I am made of stardust.
I am a star.

I shine bright every day.
When I ask for help, I always get the help I need.
I have a super day every day.
I respect others and others respect me.
It feels good to use my manners.
When other people make mistakes I forgive them quickly.
When I make mistakes I forgive myself quickly.
Just like the clouds clear when it stops raining, bad times don't last forever. The Sun always shines brighter.
I feel calm and peaceful.
I can be whatever I want to be.
I love dreaming big with my imagination.
I love my body, my hair, my skin, my eyes and my nose.
I am perfect as I am.
I love being me.
Smiling makes me feel happy.
I am always super healthy.
I have everything I need.
I am always safe.
I always do my best.
I believe in myself.
I am loved.
I am smart.
I feel so happy like it's my birthday every day.

I am brave.
I can do anything.
I think positive thoughts.
My mind is powerful.
I sleep deeply every night.
I am so kind to others and I am kind to myself.
I have so many people that love me.
I love my friends and my friends love me.
I can create anything.
I am a creative genius.
I am the painter of my life.
What I feel is important.
I love having fun.
There is always more fun ahead.
I say thank you for all the wonderful things in my life.
Thank you.
Thank you.
Thank you.
I say thank you for all the exciting things in my future.
Thank you.
Thank you.
Thank you.
I am perfect as I am.
I'm a supper happy super kid.
I play well with others.
I am very special.

I am unique.
There is only one of me in the whole world.
I have so much exciting energy.
I love learning new things.
I'm a fast learner.
I am more than enough just as I am.
I am important.
I am worth of all great things.
I deserve all great things.
I sleep deeply every night.
Great things flow to me.
I'm a great listener.
People listen to me.
I am blessed.
The world needs me.
I have a brilliant brain.
I am growing up to be happy and healthy.
Everything always goes so well for me.
I am generous.
I am helpful.
I am kind to others and I am kind to myself.
I have so many people that love me.
Sharing is caring.
I can use my imagination to create great things.
I sleep deeply every night.
I believe I am great.
I tell the truth.

I speak kind words.
I make good choices.
I feel warm and fuzzy on the inside.
Healthy food makes my body feel good.
I stand up tall and I sit up straight.
I am proud of who I am.
I am full of amazing ideas.
I feel grateful for all the fun things and people in the world.
I love our beautiful planet Earth.
I love the trees, the clouds, the sun and the breeze.
The trees, birds and animals are my friends.
I love all the wonderful animals on Earth.
I love sharing our planet with so many interesting people.
I sleep deeply every night like I'm on a fluffy cloud.
I can make my dreams come true.
I can choose to be happy at any time.
I am free.
I am made of stardust.
I am a star.
I shine bright every day.
When I ask for help, I always get the help I need.
I have a super day every day.
I respect others and others respect me.
It feels good to use my manners.

When other people make mistakes I forgive them quickly.

When I make mistakes I forgive myself quickly.

Just like the clouds clear when it stops raining, bad times don't last forever. The Sun always shines brighter.

I feel calm and peaceful.

I can be whatever I want to be.

I love dreaming big with my imagination.

I love my body, my hair, my skin, my eyes and my nose.

I am perfect as I am.

I love being me.

Smiling makes me feel happy.

I am always super healthy.

I have everything I need.

I am always safe.

I always do my best.

I believe in myself.

I am loved.

I am smart.

I feel so happy like it's my birthday every day.

I am brave.

I can do anything.

I think positive thoughts.

My mind is powerful.

I sleep deeply every night.

I am so kind to others and I am kind to myself.
I have so many people that love me.
I love my friends and my friends love me.
I can create anything.
I am a creative genius.
I am the painter of my life.
What I feel is important.
I love having fun.
There is always more fun ahead.
I say thank you for all the wonderful things in my life.
Thank you.
Thank you.
Thank you.
I say thank you for all the exciting things in my future.
Thank you.
Thank you.
Thank you.
I am perfect as I am.
I'm a supper happy super kid.
I play well with others.
I am very special.
I am unique.
There is only one of me in the whole world.
I have so much exciting energy.
I love learning new things.
I'm a fast learner.

I am more than enough just as I am.
I am important.
I am worth of all great things.
I deserve all great things.
I sleep deeply every night.

CONCLUSION

Thank you so much for reading *Bedtime Meditations For Kids.*

I hope this book has heled you have lots of wonderful dreams and amazing nights of sleep.

If you ever find yourself stressed out, angry, overwhelmed or sad you can always refer to the teachings of this book and re read it again.

If you enjoyed this book and if it has helped you have a better night's sleep, be sure to leave a thoughtful review on Amazon of how this book has helped you. This is so more kids like you can have amazing sleeps every night!

Thank you again for reading this book and I wish you all the love, happiness and amazing nights of sleep ahead!

Bedtime Sleep Meditations For Children

Guided Night Time Short Stories To Help Toddlers & Kids Fall Asleep At Night, Relax, And Have Beautiful Dreams

Author: Sleepy Willow

Do not listen to this audiobook while driving or operating machinery.

INTRODUCTION

Thank you for listening and choosing *Bedtime Sleep Meditations For Children.*

In this magical and wonderful book, you will be taken on many adventures and listen to wonderful stories that will help you to fall asleep peacefully every night. I hope that you and your children will have hours of fun listening to these stories. Each story in this book will be entertaining and will have small lessons that your child can learn from. You will learn many skills that can help you relax your mind and body, so you have the most amazing sleep every night. Each story contains valuable lessons while relieving stress. Each story will empower you and your children to improve your self-confidence and self-esteem. You will learn how to deal with your emotions better and communicate them more effectively.

Children who experience lots of nightmares might be scared to fall asleep at night and might have a hard time relaxing at night because they are afraid of scary dreams. This book will help you combat and get rid of those fears. Each story will help you feel more relaxed, calm, loved, and completely safe. You have nothing to worry about from now on.

After you have brushed your teeth, combed your hair, and put on nice comfortable pajamas, it's time for you to snuggle down in bed and get ready for sleep. You can now pick any story to help you relax and drift off to an amazing sleep.

Make sure you listen to each story and follow along. Each story has a relaxing meditation to help you get cozy and comfortable for a good night's sleep.

Are you ready to begin your bedtime meditation stories? Choose any story to begin your adventure now!

CHAPTER 1

The Confident Mermaid Adventure

Hello and welcome.

I am so happy you are here to enjoy this guided meditation.

This bedtime story takes place on an island of paradise off Hawaii's coast, where the water is so pure and sparkles and shines with so much beauty.

Mythical mermaid people live here in the beautiful underwater kingdom.

You will meet a lovely princess mermaid.

She is a little shy but very friendly and kind.

My voice will guide you safely along a fantastic journey of confidence in these beautiful ocean waters of the Hawaiian Islands.

You will journey through coral reef gardens and will experience some incredible mermaid magic.

You and your mermaid princess friend will discover how to feel wonderfully confident and free to be your happiest selves as you settle in and begin this guided bedtime sleep meditation.

You may now gently close your eyes.

Start to imagine this exceptional, wonderful, and dreamy paradise in the tropical islands of Hawaii.

You are next to beautiful swaying palm trees and hibiscus flowers in a lush green jungle.

You can also see the most beautiful and bluest ocean you have ever seen.

Take a deep breath in and a long calm breath out.

Allow yourself to breathe a little more deeply now as you allow yourself to relax into this sleep meditation.

One of the islands in Hawaii contains a hidden cove. This is a private beach with gorgeous white sands and a tiny little bay.

This place is secret from the outside world.

No tourists and no fishermen have ever been here before.

This is the magical, mystical cove of peace.

It is a safe haven for mermaid people to relax on dry land.

The waves gently flow onto the shore, and the ocean is shimmering in the moonlight.

You can see all of the stars and the galaxies from right here where you are standing.

There is a cool, refreshing breeze across the water and makes the palm trees rustle so softly.

You feel so amazing, grateful, and special to be here in this beautiful paradise.

You feel your body happily relax here as you just walk along the sand.

Dip your toes into the pure ocean water.

You have heard about the legend of mermaids and would very much like to meet one.

You then spot a beautiful spiral shell on the shore and hold it up to your ear.

You can hear the sound of the ocean from within the shell.

You start to make a special wish to see a real-life mermaid.

Suddenly glittering in the moonlight, a mermaid pops her head out of the water and swims onto shore not too far from you.
She has big green eyes with long shiny red hair.
She is decorated with beautiful seashell jewelry and has a smooth turquoise tail.
Wow, this is so amazing!
You are now filled with joy.
You walk closer slowly to meet this mermaid.
Mermaids can sometimes be very shy to humans.
She does seem a little shy as she just studies your face curiously.
It is as though she has never seen a human up close and personal before.
You give a gentle wave and smile.
You sit next to her in the sand and introduce yourself.
You explain that you are so happy to meet her.
She shyly introduces herself as Natasha, the mermaid princess.
Even though she is of royalty, she is still timid.
You explain to her that this is perfectly fine.
It is normal, and everyone feels shy from time to time, particularly when meeting new people or when in new situations.
Sometimes what can help is to sometimes pretend to feel more confident than you may actually feel inside.

You explain that everything in our life is a reflection of us, just like a mirror.

If we look scared and anxious and shy with our bodies, other people are more likely to reflect back to us those same feelings, but if we take a deep breath and relax our bodies, smile, and love, we will look and feel confident and friendly.

Then people will reflect back to us happiness, kindness, friendliness, and love.

Natasha looks down in the water and sees her reflection looking back at her in the moonlight.

She smiles and seems surprised and happy when she sees her reflection also smiles back at her.

She asks if you would like to see where she lives.

You nod your head, and then she sprinkled some gold dust which magically gives you a mermaid tail.

Your tail is rainbow-colored with pinks, purples, and blues all blending in together so beautifully.

The scales on your tail sparkle and reflect all the different colors of the rainbow.

Wow it looks so magical and gorgeous.

Natasha then sprinkles some more gold dust onto you for you to be able to breathe underwater.

You feel so incredibly excited now as you follow Natasha.

She dives into the ocean, and you both go swimming so fast with your new tail.
You start diving and dipping joyfully through the clear and pure ocean water.
You are looking forward to meeting all the sea creatures and exploring her palace.

You both swim past a coral reef with dolphins, and you hold their fins and glide through the water.
You give a turtle a high five that swims past you.
Then you swim and play with a clownfish.
Then you start to see other mermaid people and Natasha talks to lots of people.
Wow she is so kind and so loveable.
Lots of sea creatures and mermaid people love her very much.

Natasha should never forget this when meeting new people or when she is in a new place with a different environment.
She is so liked and loved already, and this is definitely something to feel confident about.
She laughs and then thanks you so much for helping her to see this.

Sometimes everyone is so busy worrying about themselves that they probably don't notice they look shy.

You swim with Natasha some more through her beautiful underwater kingdom.

You swim past mermaids brushing their hair, and you see mermen working out with big shells.

You see merbabies just sleeping or playing around.

You see others reading ancient books about Atlantis, playing cards, and storytelling.

They are all too absorbed in their own lives to care about whether she looks shy or not.

Natasha laughs and thinks that she has been worried about things that are totally unnecessary for a long time.

You both laugh, and you both let go of the fear of what people may think of you.

You both now immediately look and feel so much more confident in yourselves.

Wow this is so wonderful.

You ask Natasha curiously what divine talents she has that she thinks are very special?

She tells you she loves to make beautiful jewelry.

She smiles so widely when you explain that this something to really be proud of and confident about.

You think to yourself of your very own unique talents too.

As you both swim through the beautiful coral gardens, Natasha tells you that sometimes she feels a lot of pressure to act like a princess.
This makes her very self-conscious at times.
You suggest to her to just be herself and love who she really is.
Then everyone will love her honesty and reflect it back to her.
Mermaid people are all different and wonderful in their own unique ways.
It is so exhausting and unnatural not to be yourself.
Just be who you are and let your light shine to the world.

You both laugh together now, and both let go of this idea that you're not allowed to be your authentic selves because in truth and reality, you have every permission to be your true selves now.
Everyone else is taken, so be yourself.
You both now immediately look more happy and relaxed.

It is okay to be quieter than other people.
You don't have to be the loudest person.
That is perfectly natural and normal because you may not want to be the center of attention all the time.
There is nothing to feel shy about as it is normal and healthy to be a quiet person.
You are just as wonderful, amazing, valuable, and interesting as those who have loud voices.
You can both be quietly confident because this is a beautiful and powerful thing.

Natasha swims around in a happy circle, smiles, and thanks you endlessly for your wise advice.
You also tell Natasha to look people in the eye when talking to them so you can really connect with them.
It gets easier the more you practice and makes you feel super confident.
Also, it is excellent manners to look people in the eyes when you are speaking with them.
She thanks you again for your wisdom.
In return, she gives you a massive white pearl that is round and glimmering beautifully in the crystal-clear ocean waters.
You are feeling so happy and confident now.

You swim around with your rainbow tail and stretch your arms out and take up as much space as you can.
I am confident.
Natasha laughs and does the same.
You both share your positive affirmations with each other, which helps you feel super confident.
I am safe.
I am smart.
I am loved.
I am healthy.
I am enough.
I am worthy.
I am important.
I can do anything.

A group of mermaids from another kingdom visits you both and swims up to you and Natasha.
They ask you both for directions to the palace.
You and Natasha both smile, look them in the eyes, and gesture with your arms to clearly point the way.
They all smile back at you and Natasha, and they thank you both and swim off in their way.
Natasha turns to you so happily.
She has now become so confident, and you feel even more confident now.

Just watching her apply everything you both have learned about feeling confident.
Awesome job and well done.

You may wish to celebrate her confidence and your confidence as well by swimming through the coral palace and through the pure ocean water with dolphins and fishes.
Enjoy the colorful coral garden palace and just love being in the beautiful and peaceful paradise.
Whatever your heart desires, you can now do it with confidence, happiness, and ease.
You are feeling so very special, joyful, and wonderful about the new possibilities in life.
You now have a friendly smile and a confident heart.
You accept and love who you truly are.
My voice is going to leave you soon to sleep deeply now.
Relax into the most peaceful and happiest sleepy dreams.
I wish you every ounce of happiness and love.
May you enjoy your blissful and sweet dreams.

CHAPTER 2

The Magic Carpet Ride

Hello and welcome to this guided, enchanted adventure story.

Very soon, you will love and enjoy having your very own magic carpet ride.

My voice will guide you happily and safely through this guided sleep meditation to a whole new wonderful world for you to relax and to use your wonderful imagination.

You will enjoy and take a magic carpet ride full of delight and make some fantastic new friends.

You will feel so free and happy.

Anything is possible when we choose a new point of view.

You can let go of negative thoughts and rise above them to be positive.

Life is so much more fun this way.

When we let go of negativity, the world is so exciting and such a magical place to see.

As you snuggle under the covers and get really cozy, you may close your eyes now and enjoy the darkness behind your eyelids.

You feel your body start to relax, and you feel little tingles of excitement as you feel that there is lots of magic in the air.

You know that something wonderful and amazing is about to happen.

Now take a deep breath in and out.

Feel so happy as you imagine what life could be like.

You can hear a slight rustle at your window.

You feel a rush of joy because you can see the most outstanding real-life magic carpet hovering and floating in the moonlight waiting just for you.

The moonlight is shining down with a safe and loving energy.

You step onto the magic carpet, and you are pleasantly surprised by how soft it feels under your bare feet.

You sit down and run your hands over the carpet's fluffy soft fabric.

It makes you feel warm and safe inside.

You can also see golden tassels hanging down from each corner of the carpet.

The magic carpet is woven from richly colorful Persian fabrics and has intricate designs.

You can see pictures from many legends and stories throughout history.

Wow how fascinating!

You sense that this is a very ancient and special magic carpet.

You feel so blessed to be riding on it.

As soon as you think this positive and grateful thought, the carpet lifts up and hovers in the air before taking off.

Now you are flying through the shimmering starlight.

Suddenly you find yourself on the carpet flying over the beautiful Arabian desert.

You can see the sand glittering a little in the moonlight.

You take a deep breath in and feel that there is so much space here.

It is so quiet and peaceful and really beautiful.

Now all of a sudden, the magic carpet ripples, which was seems to be excitement.
Then it rises about in the air.
Your carpet now catches a gust of wind and rushes up into the air.
Oh my!
This is so much fun!
Anything you wish is its command.
You feel a warm, calm breeze across your face and through your hair.
You rush through the night sky.
The happier and loved you feel, the more you appreciate and be grateful for what you see around you and in your heart, the faster the carpet flies and the higher it goes.
Wow this is so much fun.
You can now see a gorgeous palace shimmering in the starlight.
It has enormous impressive domed-shaped rooftops made of marble and gold.
It has beautiful wavy designs and looks like the desert sands inspired the design.
The palace is so beautiful.
You happily wish there were some friends to see and enjoy this with you and share this adventure.

As you and your magic carpet fly closer to the fantastic palace, you can see two people standing in front under a giant palm tree.

As you fly closer, you can see it is a girl and a boy.

They are smiling up at you and waving.

You sense that they are good kind people.

The carpet flies down and hovers in front of them.

The boy and the girl both look very familiar to you.

It is as though maybe you have seen them somewhere else before.

You introduce yourself, and you meet Jasmine.

She is a kind-hearted and intelligent young Arabian princess.

She has lovely dark and long hair.

She climbs onto your magic carpet, and then you meet a funny and clever Arabian prince who tells you his name is Ali.

He then happily climbs onto the carpet to ride with you as well.

As the three of you ride together and fly up on your magic carpet, Princess Jasmine gives you a wonderful and royal tour of the palace in the sky.

She points out the gardens, the pools, and the gorgeous buildings from the sky above as you fly.

Then a city of fantastic architecture appears in the distance.

The three of you look down and admire the stunning art and unique swirls and spirals of so many beautiful colors.

You can see reds, purples, blues, turquoise, and greens.

These colorful designs are celebrating the artistic culture of the Persian empire throughout history.

Wow.

What a magnificent and wonderful city this is.

As you three continue to fly over the desert land and above huge sand dunes, Ali tells jokes and makes you all laugh.

As you laugh, you look up, and you can see the stars shimmering and twinkling in the sky.

You can see the stars so clearly, and they look so incredible.

There are many more stars in the universe than grains of sand on Earth, Jasmine said.

The whole sky is shimmering with the glorious starlight.

You point up at shooting star beaming across the sky.

You all cheer with excitement.
Wow you feel so happy.
You now promise to let go of all negativity and always choose positive thoughts and positive feelings because then your life can be like a magical adventure.

You are just enjoying the calm, cool breeze flying through the night sky on your magic carpet with your fun and amazing new friends.
Suddenly a beautiful sight appears before you.
You see a desert oasis of aqua blue pools of water.
It looks like a glowing jewel in the desert sands.

This peaceful and beautifully lush Oasis looks like a mystical and enchanting mirage.
As you get closer, you can see it is real.
Wow it is so breathtakingly beautiful.
This is truly amazing.

You can see friendly camels drinking at the water's edge of the Oasis.

Then look up and start smiling at you all with their big funny teeth and gummy smiles.
You have never ridden a camel before.
Maybe now is the time.
It is entirely up to you.

You can go anywhere on your magic carpet with your new friends.
You can ride across the middle east, Africa, Asia, Europe, or even Oceania.
You can travel anywhere your heart desires.
You can go to a whole new world of possibilities of shining and sparkling dreams.
You can create the most positive and amazing ideas and exploring the wonderful world on your magic carpet.
You feel so blissfully happy and peacefully powerful because you now know that you can create positive thoughts instantly.
You can make the most beautiful things into reality and experiences for yourself and others.
You can choose to think positive thoughts which keep you soaring high and moving forward fast both on your magic carpet and in your life.

Now our adventure is starting to end.

I want you to always keep riding high, thinking positively, and having fun on your enchanted journey.

I want you to keep having fun on your magic carpet ride for as long as you wish in your happiest and dreamiest sleep.

I wish you all the happiness in the world and good night.

CHAPTER 3

The Fairy Forest

Welcome children to experience your imagination and happiness where we will focus only on feeling good.
Are you ready for this adventure?
Close your eyes now and make yourself really comfortable.
Stretch your whole body out and let your arms, legs, and belly relax.

Take a big deep breath in through your nose and slowly and gently breathe out through your mouth.
Again take a deep breath in through your nose and slowly and gently breathe out through your mouth.
One more time, deep breath in through your nose and slowly and gently breathe out through your mouth.

Amazing.

You're doing fantastic.

Now imagine that you are walking along fresh green soft grass with your bare feet.

The grass is cool, refreshing, soft, and a little ticklish under your feet.

You feel so calm and so relaxed.

This is called grounding.

This keeps your energy planted in the ground, and you feel connected to the earth and to all of nature.

Our planet earth has an amazing and very special energy, and you are now connected to it.

Now imagine looking up into the night sky and seeing the beautiful stars sparkling across the sky.

You notice that one star is a bit brighter than all of the others.

It is shining the brightest out of all of them.

You can see it twinkling as it shines its light down onto you.

Suddenly a huge beam of light shines down from the star around your whole body.

This is such a beautiful silvery-white light that is glowing all around you.

You are now shining like the brightest star.

This starlight is made out of pure love and is keeping you safe and happy.

This light is always around you.

You feel so relaxed and peaceful.

Amazing.

You are doing so great.

Now imagine you're standing at the edge of the enchanted forest in the starlight.

You can see a path glistening between the trees shining down and invites you to walk along and follow it.

You step along this magical path made up of green grass that is so soft under your feet.

You feel very safe and happy here in this ancient forest.

You have a feeling and sense that the trees here are wise and old and friendly.

Here there are lots of lovely animals waiting to meet you.

You look around you and see that the trees have what looks like faces in their ancient trunks.

They all look they are smiling at you so friendly.

Suddenly a fairy flies by your face and starts to just hover in front of you.

Wow it's a real-life fairy!

Their wings look so delicate like a butterfly, and it has a golden glow around itself.

It smiles with you with such a kind smile and then darts off further into the forest.

As you follow this twisting and turning path, you admire the huge colorful flowers growing extra big and beautiful because the forest is enchanted with glorious vines.

The vines have flowers hanging down along the pathway.

The plants and trees seem to just be sparkling.

As you look closer, you realize that there are glow worms and fireflies and fairy lights shimmering everywhere.

This forest is just so pure, and you feel so safe, happy, and loved here.

You now can hear faint sounds of enchanting music drifting through the beautiful forest trees.

You follow the sound of music and the path as you come to a clearing.

In front of you is the most gorgeous scenery.

There is a perfect circle of soft green grass glowing silver in the moonlight with mushrooms and red-spotted toadstools forming a circle in the grass.

The fairies are in a circle smiling and waving to you and welcoming you into their clearing.

You see elves playing bagpipes, flutes, fiddles, and harps, creating some magical music.

Now the fairies and pixies are all dancing and fluttering in between trees and toadstools.
They all wave at you and invite you to join them.
You dance and twirl with them in the soft grass.
Wow this is so much fun!
You feel so free as you laugh about and dance to the mystical happy music.
You now have some time to just enjoy yourself in the secret enchanted part with your new fairy, elf, and pixie friends.

The moon is high in the sky shining, and the magical music starts to fade away as the elves, pixies, and fairies dance off into the forest.
You sense that it is time to leave the clearing.
You are feeling so joyful, peaceful, and alive.
You walk back along the moonlit path on the soft green grass back through the big wise old trees.
Past the gorgeous flowers.
Fairies are sitting on the flowers and smile at you and wave goodbye.
As you walk past, two glowing fairies fly and hover in front of you.
They smile at you with delight, wave, and dart off into the forest.

You follow the path back the way you came twisting and turning through the Enchanted forest.
You feel so safe and loved in the pure moonshine.
You are so relaxed as you take one step after another, walking slowly between the trees.

Your whole body feels heavy and peaceful.
You notice how quiet and still the forest has become.
All of the creatures have now gone to sleep.
You see fairies sleeping in the beautiful flowers.
You also see them sleeping under the giant mushrooms and sleeping in the tree houses.
Everything is so calm and peaceful as the forest falls fast asleep.
You walk to the edges of the trees and then straight into the bed where you sleep all snug and cozy under the covers.
Your whole body is calm and heavy and relaxed.
You feel so special and so happy.
You know you can visit the enchanted forest anytime you wish.
Sweet dreams.

CHAPTER 4

Rapunzel and Believing

Once upon a time, in a dreamy land far, far away, there is a long blonde-haired girl in a tower with no stairway.

This girl is named Rapunzel, and her hair is like gold. She is trapped by an evil spell by someone cold and jealous.

Tonight you will visit Rapunzel and help her realize something that can only be discovered with a happy heart and a mind that is wise.

When we believe in ourselves we can do anything and find within ourselves the answers to be free from everything.

Welcome to this lovely enchanted sleep-guided meditation story.

It will lead you to your happiest and most wonderful relaxation.

We will journey safely together into this land of magical dreams.

My voice will guide you gently to this land across rainbows and moonlight beams.

Are you ready to meet Rapunzel and enjoy this beautiful fairytale story?

As you help the princess, you will also discover your own glory and improve your self-beliefs.

Close your eyes now and gently take a big deep breath in and out.

You're doing fantastic.

Your muscles are starting to relax and unwind.

Now breathe in a little more deeply and settle in peacefully with ease to this guided sleep meditation story.

Now you can easily picture the moonlight glittering down through your window surrounding your whole body in the pure energy of love and safety.

It is such a gorgeous silvery glow.

Your heart swells up with happiness as the beams of light sparkle down, and the rainbow appears in the nighttime sky.

This colorful enchanted night rainbow will transport you safely to the land of fairy tales.

You find yourself relaxing more as the light of the rainbow surrounds you allowing your thoughts to drift.

Images start appearing but not too fast and not too slow.

It is just right for you.

Simply relax as my voice drifts along the rainbow with you.

You drift along with it through the glittering night rainbow into the land of dreams and fairy tales.

You now happily find yourself at the other end of the rainbow in an open flower field of daisies.

Snowcapped mountains of pine trees surround you.

You look around you, and you cannot see anyone else or any buildings here as far as your eyes can see.

The air is so fresh and healthy here.

The air is a little cool, but the sun on your skin feels warm.

Take a deep breath in and enjoy the lovely fragrance of flowers and fresh Jasmine and lavender around you.

You can see bumblebees just buzzing lazily around the flowers of tulips and daisies.

You admire what a beautiful place this is.

This meadow has an energy that is so pure and clean, and healthy.

You run through the meadow with your arms outstretched and twirl around so freely.

You grab some daises and wear them in your hair.

Now while you are enjoying this, you hear a lovely voice singing an old song drifting through the mountain air.

You notice the beautiful singing seems to be coming from behind some trees.

You now notice there is a tower standing all by itself. As you begin to walk closer, you can see the tower has a fairytale-style room at the top.

There is a pointer on top of the tower to reflect the sun, and seems to sparkle with like a magical light.

How interesting.

You walk around the tower and notice a beautiful ivy vine growing around the outside.

There doesn't appear to be a door either.

How strange.

The lovely singing is much louder now.

You can see the window at the top of the tower starts to open, and the gentle singing stops.

A beautiful face looks down at you from the window.

The girl in the tower just looks at you and studies you curiously.

Then she smiles happily and gives you a friendly wave.

You instantly feel that you will get along really well and become friends.

You realize this must be Rapunzel.

She happily lets her hair down for you to climb up the tower and meet her enormous silky golden blonde hair.

It looks like golden strands all spun together and is cascading down to where you are standing on the meadow ground below.

You easily climb up her braided hair, which feels like a smooth golden rope glowing in the sun all the way into the window.

At the top of the tower, you can see the meadow, valleys, and mountains.

The view from up here is breathtaking.

Although the tower feels really small with just one room with a bed, a harp, and a bookcase of old fairy tales.

There is also a teeny tiny room to the side of the tower, which is a dressing room for the princess to sit and brush her hair.

She tells you that she passes the time by singing and playing with the beautiful and cheery birds which comes to visit her at her window sill.

You ask Rapunzel why she feels trapped here.

She tells you an evil person casted a spell on her, and there doesn't appear to be a way out for her.

Rapunzel tells you sadly that a lovely prince used to visit her but was not able to save her.

You ask Rapunzel why she doesn't break the spell and save herself.

Maybe she just feels more trapped than she actually is.

There must be a way out.

She looks at you with wide-eyed amazement because she has never thought of this before.

You suggest and explain to Rapunzel that the only power a person has over you is what you allow to be true.

What if you're only ever trapped in your own mind and that anything and everything is actually possible.

There is a solution for everything, and the answers are always within us if we just calm our minds, listen to our hearts, and believe in ourselves.

With amazement and excitement, Rapunzel nods her head happily and agrees with you wholeheartedly.

She understands now that all she has to do is believe in herself and trust her heart.

This spell won't hold any power over her.

All that really matters is the surprise and realization that she starts to think about her freedom.

Then a friendly and cheerful bluebird flies in and rests on the window sill carrying a stick from the pine trees in its beak.

Rapunzel looks at the bluebird, then looks at you, and her eyes light up with joy.

She just came up with a brilliant idea.

Rapunzel unravels her glorious hair and tells you to climb back down that tower.

So you climb all the way down her golden hair and step down gently into the meadow.

As you look up, you watch her escape plan unfold.

Rapunzel grabs the stick from the bluebird and jams it into the window's hinges, creating what looks like a hook.

She ties the end of her hair around the stick and then, with a confident grin, climbs down her hair.

She is working her way down from the top of the tower to the bottom.

Wow Rapunzel is saving herself!

She scales down the tower quickly, happily, and cheerfully.

She loves her newfound confidence and self-belief.

When she reaches the meadow ground, she gives her hair a good yank, and the rest of her hair falls into the meadow.

You are surprised to see Rapunzel rolling around in the grass, laughing with happiness and joy.

She actually freed herself.
You can't help but laugh as well.
It feels so good to laugh as you realize how important and easy it is to believe in ourselves.
Rapunzel finds it so funny that the answer was there all along with her.
The so-called spell was only something she was allowing to be true.
She had the power to break it the whole time.
All she had to do was believe in herself and know that positive energy and our inner spirit are always more powerful.
Just be watching Rapunzel learning this lesson with her makes your confidence rise.
You think to yourself how great it feels to laugh about it as you feel your confidence raised.
You believe in yourself more now too.
Any previously held fears feel like distant memories that now mean nothing.
Rapunzel runs through the field of daisies and tulips with her arms outstretched.
You run through the field with her as you both twirl around and announce to the world that from now on, you will write your own stories and live your happiest, fullest and freest life, sing, have a voice to share with the world, and to share all of your unique talents to the world.

Rapunzel thanks you endlessly for helping her to realize the truth.

Do you feel even more inspired to do the same in your own life?

To believe in yourself and live freely and joyfully?

Trusting that there are always happy solutions in any situation.

When we believe in ourselves and in our own power within anything is possible.

What a fantastic adventure you're having in the land of dreams and fairy tales.

Learning to believe in yourself just like how Rapunzel did.

You are feeling so wonderfully happy and also sleepy and tired.

It has been a very big day, and you are not sure if this is all a dream.

You may wish to keep exploring the beautiful relaxing nature around you of the flower meadow and the snow-capped mountains with your friend Rapunzel.

Your whole body has drifted deeper and deeper now into this guided meditation.

You are in a beautiful dreamland now as you switch off and go with the flow to my voice to your most relaxing and blissful sleep.

My voice will leave you soon because you are loving drifting into your happiest and most confident and peaceful dreams now.

Knowing now that you believe in yourself that you can be and do anything.

As my voice fades away, you are feeling so happy, loved, cozy and confident.

Since you believe in yourself, you now know that you can explore your happiest fairytale dream adventures anytime you wish.

Sweet Dreams.

CHAPTER 5

The Sleepy Animal Kingdom

Gently close your eyes and stretch out your body.
Make sure you are in a completely comfortable position, so you can relax and start to dream.
The wonderful meditation magic can happen when you are almost asleep.
Take a deep breath in and a calm breath out.
One more time, take a deep breath in and a long calm breath out.
That's wonderful.
It is so exciting that the animals have invited you to play with them tonight.
As you start to relax more and more, imagine the starlight streaming in through your window.
Now, imagine this glorious starlight surrounding your whole body.

This divine light is the energy of pure love and it always keeps you safe.

To your surprise and amazement, you start to see grass growing on the floor.
Plants are sprouting up out of nowhere.
Your cupboard becomes a huge tree.
The light becomes a full moon.
Vines start to hang down from the ceiling.
Your room disappears around you and green leaves start to grow.
Exotic flowers start to bloom and the most beautiful tropical plants you have ever seen start to appear everywhere.

You notice that your bed is no longer a bed but it is now a soft patch of spotted mushrooms.

A sloth swings down from a branch and winks at you.
You instantly realize you are now in a sleepy jungle.
The moonlight shines down through the trees bathing the sleepy jungle in the silvery light of love.

You look around and you see that everything glows in the moonshine and looks magical.

With your bare feet, you step onto the soft fluffy grass.

You instantly feel safe and connected to the Earth here.

A feeling and sense of fun starts to dance within your heart.

This is your special adventure!

What animals do you want to meet tonight?

A monkey with a huge grin and a long curly tail swings over to you and waves you to climb up the vine.

You discover you can climb so easily just like a monkey.

You start to swing through the trees with your new monkey friend.

You can feel the fresh night breeze on your face.

As you catch and swing from the vines, you feel so free.

You spot some gorillas on the jungle floor relaxing next to very big plants.

These friendly gorillas smile to you and you climb down to meet them.
They show you how to walk like a gorilla on your knuckles and teach you how to be proud of yourself.
They show you how to peel bananas in the best way possible.

Now you see some eyes looking at you through the plants.
A black panther appears between the leaves and walks towards you.

The panther has a beautiful black coat.
It is glistening in the moonlight.
The panther nods at you and invites you to climb on its back.

You hop on and pet its smooth fur.

It starts running through the trees.

The panther is running so fast.

Running past huge exotic flowers and plants.
You feel so happy and light as you race through the jungle on your super-fast panther friend.

The sleepy jungle has the friendliest animals in the world.
They are so happy here and they live in perfect harmony with each other.
You start to hear the sound of flowing water.

Now, you see a jungle stream of crystal-clear water.
Your panther friend stops by the stream and you hop off and pet its soft black coat.
You look at the water sparkling in the moonlight as it bubbles along and into a pond.
There are huge gorgeous lily pads with pink flowers and big green frogs sitting on them in this huge pond.

The frog smiles up at you and invites you onto its lily pad.
You step onto the green pad and from one lily pad to another across the water.
Wow this is so amazing!

You are as light as a feather and can jump far like a frog, hopping over lily pads.

A brightly colored toucan flies down from a nearby tree and gestures you to follow it.

You look up at the toucan's big beak and dazzling tropical feathers.
You think wow such an incredible bird.
You let the toucan guide you the rest of the way.
As you walk along the green soft fluffy grass, it flies just above you, so you know where to go through the sleepy forest.

You feel that it is taking you through this sleepy jungle to a very special place.

Now, you arrive at the coziest, dreamiest, and sleepiest place in the sleepy jungle.
You have arrived at a sleeping cave of a tiger.

This is a safe, dark, and secret cave.
It is hidden between the sleeping sloths.

You crawl quietly inside the cave and you see colors of orange and black.
You see a striped tiger relaxing happily in the cave.
You lie down next to its soft, warm body.
It is breathing slowly and heavily in

And out.

Sleepy Willow

In

And out.

You feel so safe and so calm.

Resting next to this big friendly tiger are two birds laying down near you with their wings folded.
You can see out of the cave entrance to the nearby branches are sloths sleeping lazily in the trees above.

The entire jungle now starts to rest.
The moon hides behind some clouds and seems like it is sleeping too.
Your eyes now feel very heavy and your breathing gets deeper and deeper.
You close your eyes.

You feel so cozy and warm and special.
You feel yourself drifting off.

Into your happiest dreams.

As you sleep deeply now in the tiger's sleeping cave in the sleepy jungle, you feel so happy and so blessed.
You know you are so safe here and so loved by all the jungle animals around you as you sleep even more deeply now.

With pure peace in your heart, you know that you are so very special.

You feel so wonderful exactly as you are.
Your animal friends of the sleepy jungle are waiting just for you.

You can visit any time you wish.

Sleepy jungle dreams.

Have you ever met a lion before?
A real lion in the wild?
Well, lions get up at night when all of the other animals in the savanna start to sleep at night.

Tonight Leo the magnificent lion king and Leon his fun and playful cub, are inviting you to roam about freely with them.
Joining them as they like to explore and have the dreamiest and the most wonderful nighttime adventure that you can possibly imagine, before you drift off to sleep.

Now, as you snuggle in and start to feel cozy and comfortable, you can close your eyes and show your lion friends how you are.

So very quiet and being totally still.

These sleepy lions always know what is going on around them by listening carefully to the sounds of the breeze and remaining so very still.

They pay attention with all of their lion senses because even when lions look like they're lazing about so happily, maybe even seeming to be sound asleep.

Don't be fooled.

Those sleepy lions are always ready to pounce and prowl and maybe even roar.

Sometimes even just for fun to surprise other sleepy animals around them.

It is also to remind everyone who really is king of the sleepy savanna.

I think you are going to enjoy and be surprise tonight on your very own marvelous dream adventure.

You may feel very excited inside and even might find yourself starting to dream away.

Dreaming of wide green open plains.

You see with your mind's eye, the tall and strong baobab trees.

You see so many interesting and wonderful rock formations.

You can also easily see the bright and clear moon.
It is high in the sky and everything glowing in the moonshine is enchanted by a silvery moonlight that sparkles beautifully.
You now hear all the peaceful calming sounds of this place including the soft running water from a gentle stream.

You now peer through the clear moonlight.
You see two amazing animals drinking water from the stream.
One of them runs over to you and how you can make out a young lion's face.

It is a lion with friendly eyes and a mischievous grin.
This young lion introduces himself as Leon.
Now his father Leo walks over to you looking proud.
He has a majestic mane that looks like a rock star.

He has such a great proud posture.
Leo holds out his massive paw for you to shake as he tells you his name.
He is king Leo the pride of the land.
King Leo and Leon smiles warmly at you and you instantly sense they are kindhearted.
You feel so safe and calm in their presence because you know they will protect you no matter what.
You feel like a soft tickly feeling from the lion fur of Leon as he nuzzles playfully into you.
He has a warm fuzzy coat.
King Leo tells you they are going to take you on a night tour of the pride lands.
It is to do night watching of the sleeping animals because they are the protectors of the sleepy savannah.
They would love for you to see some of the most fun places.
You feel so excited now.
You begin to follow the path of the stream.
With Leo prancing ahead you and Leon are hopping, skipping, tripping and jumping along.

As you follow the long relaxing flowing stream, you see it winds out to a clear open of the grassland.

Now you see before you this beautiful savannah.

It stretches out so wide and far.
You see the lovely clear water of the stream which flows into a pond.
This pond has become quite muddy and all of a sudden, you hear the funny sounds of loud snoring.
You can't quite make out where it's coming from, but you see a huge rock stuck in the mud there.

This rock suddenly moves, and you see a humongous muddy face and you realize it is a massive hippopotamus.
It is resting, snoring, and happily sleeping.

The giant sleepy hippo rolls over with an enormous snore coming from its huge nostrils.
Leo grins and very soon, he tickles the hippo's nose with a feather and the hippo blows out an even bigger snore.
It was the loudest and funniest snore you have ever heard.

The hippos wriggles a bit deeper into the mud.

Leon dips his little lion head into the goopy brown mud.
He suddenly presses his paw onto your hand.
You feel so wild and free like a lion.

You feel that you truly belong in this lion pride now.

Now having checked on the hippos, you all race out across the open grassland.
You run as fast as you possibly can, but you are no match for King Leo.
He is the fastest lion in all of the sleepy savannah.

King Leo is helping you out because you are now a part of the pride.
The king of the lions bows his strong neck down and lets you climb onto his back.

You now hold on very tight to King Leo's big Rockstar mane and fluffy fur.
He runs faster and faster with Leon running as fast alongside him.

You all race through the savannah.

You leap over many rocks and now are darting through the trees.
Everything around you becomes a blur.

After a little while, you all slow down again.
You slow down to a gentle walking pace feeling so relaxed.

The three of you arrive at the beautiful tall trees where all of the sleeping giraffes like to lay about as they rest.
Underneath the green leafy trees, you see all the giraffes peacefully curled up on the ground.

They have long necks curved around and relaxed.

They are resting so easily on their long front legs.
Every giraffe is smiling happily as you see each one snooze.
The giraffes look so funny because they are twisting their necks into strange sleeping positions.
Everyone appears to be calm and cozy.
You are sleeping so well and enjoying all of this fun relaxing happy time.
You start to notice King Leo is so powerful, proud, and compassionate.
Here you see and know that he has great respect for this circle of life.

Each and every night, he chooses to check in on his sleeping kingdom.

He makes sure they are sleeping so safe and soundly.
Feeling so blissfully protected as they sleep.

You now see and understand Leon loves learning from his father and likes to have fun along the way.
As you continue to explore more, you will be surprised to discover that the lions watch over the entire circle of life every night.
They watch over the sleepy elephants to the sleeping eagles.
From the relaxing meer cats to all of the sleeping zebras.
Every animal in the sleepy savannah are all looked after by the protective King Leo.

Now this sleepy restful night adventure is all done now.
You feel such amazing joy in your heart.
You feel so happy and will have such an incredible sleep.
It is so fun and free to be a part of the lion's pride.
Together you are all traveling all the way back over the soft sleepy grasslands.

You go all the way back to the biggest rock in the savannah.
You see he has a lovely cozy and calming cave.

Here inside is the safest cave.
This is where you find the mama lion, Leon's brothers and sisters and the rest of the lion pride.
They are all now sleeping.
You are so curious but you are becoming more tired than before.
You crawl into the smooth sleepy cave with all the sleepy lions.
You lie down to sleep in the safest, softest and warmest space just for you.
This lovely cave is so dark and so cozy.
It feels so warm and safe sleeping with the wonderful pride of the lions.
You are all nestled together for a deep deep sleep.
You feel the soft fur of the sleeping lions and you feel completely safe.
You easily fall asleep.

You feel so protected and at home.
You are among the friendliest of all the lions.
You are the most special new member of the sleepy lion's pride.
Now as you relax more and more.
You continue to sleep and all you hear are the lions snoozing and relaxing.

They are so happy together.
You all enjoy a healthy restful sleep at night.

Your entire body relaxes and you sink down into a deep sleep.
You enjoy all of your positive lovely dreams of the sleepy savannah.
You continue to feel so extremely happy inside.
You wish your sweetest, coziest, and happiest lion dreams to appear.
Now the meditation adventure of the sleepy safari begins.

All you need to do is relax your body and allow your imagination to take you on the most wonderful places.
You are on a very special sleepy safari.
It is leaving you soon and you better get ready.

You close your eyes and you make sure they are very comfortable.
As you settle in, you may think about which animals you wish to see.

You take a deep breath in and a calm breath out.
Again you take a deep breath in and a long calm breath out.

You continue to breathe and you start to feel more and more relaxed.

Amazing! Your body feels all heavy and floppy now.

Now imagine you are standing on an African savannah.
Imagine there are sleepy planes all around you and as far as you can see.
The orange sun is shining brightly.
The earth feels warm under your bare feet.
You feel yourself connecting to the land here.
You are very excited and you are here for a sleepy safari.

You suddenly see a jeep cruiser driving towards you. It is in a cloud of dust and you can see the color of the jeep as it gets closer and closer.

You realize it is my tour guide.

It is coming to pick you up for your safari adventure.

The big car comes to a halt with dust swirling everywhere.

When you see who is driving it, you are very surprised.

There is a tiger behind the wheel with a safari hat.

He is wearing a Hawaiian shirt with binoculars around his neck.

He gives you a friendly smile and waves his paw to you.

He checks his clipboard and reads your name out loud.

You smile and say yes.

The tiger leans over and pushes the door open for you to climb inside.

Your tiger guide drives you super fast across the sleepy safari.

He is a casual tiger and very easy going.

He has lots of fun.

This is no ordinary safari.

He drives you up a big grassy hill and you wonder where is he leading you?
There seems to be nothing around.
Now you see over the rise from the top of the hill is the most amazing scene in front of you.

There is a beautiful valley below with a river winding along and into a big blue pond.
Huge baobab trees dodge the landscape holding water in their bulging trunks.
There are grasslands and also a green forest area that is waiting for you to explore it.
You feel so peaceful here.
It is already lots of fun to be here in Africa.
Your tiger tour guide grins at you and looks pretty impressed with himself.
He tells you that this is the secret reserve.
That only the animals know about.
You feel so lucky to be here.
There are two friendly elephants greeting you at the top of the hill.
One for you and one for the tiger.

You climb onto your new elephant friend.
You hold onto the tufted hair on its back.
Your body wobbles and jiggles all over the place.
The elephant takes huge steps and walks slowly down the hill slope.
You are now down in the valley.
You climb off your elephant.

You feel very excited and very relaxed.
All of your favorite animals were right here in their natural habitat.
This is now your special time to meet the animals.
This is your very own sleepy safari, and your tiger tour guide is right here with you.
You can go running with the cheetahs or you may wish to go swimming on vines with the monkeys.
You could climb up trees and help the tall giraffes find the very best leaves.
You can visit the hippopotamus in its muddy waterhole.
There are meer cats, zebras, gazelles and every animal you wish to see.
You have some time now to explore the valley.
You meet all the animals your heart desires.
You are starting to feel even more sleepy and ready to be in your happiest dreams.

After having so much fun with the animals, you notice the sun is setting far in the distance.

It is glowing orange and fading now.

It dips below the horizon, and moonlight is shining over the valley.

The stars have come out to play.

They twinkle so beautifully in the night sky.

There are so many stars and you see them so clearly as you gaze up in awe.

You start to feel very very sleepy.

As the stars sparkle above you, the valley starts to fade.

As you get sleepier and sleepier, it is now time to return home to bed.

You wave goodbye to the animals of the secret valley.

You wave goodbye to your tiger tour guide.

He waves his paw to you and smiles.

You can now feel that you were in a warm cozy bed.

As you sleep deeply, now there is pure joy in your heart.

You know that anything is possible.

You are so very special and completely loved.

You can dream so happy now.

The animals can't wait for you to visit them again for another meditation adventure anytime you wish.
The sweet sleepy safari.

As you settle into the most comfortable and cozy position, you gently close your eyes.
Can you imagine a very special place?
The most wonderful fun tropical jungle where all of the animals live happily in harmony with each other.
I will let you on a very little-known secret.
There is such a place called a mindful jungle hidden deep within the calming valley.
It is between peaceful mountains where the animals gather together and meditate before falling deep asleep.
They drift into the most amazing dreams.
They fall asleep so fast and so well.
All these animals always wake up feeling so refreshed before having the most fun and delightful days.
They have focused positive minds because all of your favorite animals love to do their mindful sleep meditation.
They gather together under the trees.
They are inviting you to join them right now.

It feels very enchanting because the sun has already set and the stars have come out to twinkle in the night sky.
Everyone is feeling very sleepy and ready for a cozy sleep.
You feel so lucky to be invited.

The fluffy lion begins by taking three deep breaths in and out.
The lions can only do their mighty roars with very good deep breathing.
Together you breathe in and out.
You breathe deeply, just like the gentle breeze of the jungle trees.
You are doing fantastic!
You notice the lion is very tired and his breaths became big yawns.
You can't help but to do a mighty lion yawn as well.
The next elephant relaxes his heavy body from its elephant ears all the way down to its trunk and jaw, even all the way down to its feet.
Together you relax your whole body.
You feel all heavy and sleepy like your elephant friend.

Now the elephant yawns an even bigger yawn.
You all yawn too.
This is the biggest yawn you have ever yawned before.
Now a cute monkey calms its monkey mind.
Like the adorable monkey, you observe your thoughts before letting them float away like clouds in a night sky.
The monkey snuggles into a cozy position feeling sleepier and sleepier.
It is so very relaxing.
It does a little monkey yawn and ready to dream about the funniest things.
Together just like your monkey friend, you relax your body even more ready to dream about the most wonderful things that you can imagine.
You may notice the gentle giraffe practices patience very well listening high up to the sounds of the leaves rustling in the treetops and all of the noises in the distance.
Together you tune your ears noticing many different sounds both near and far far away.
You can hear the sound of your breathing.
Perhaps you are already asleep, and the cuddly bear notices its feelings.
Deep inside with all of its bare heart and all of its many feelings are welcome here.

Together you notice your feelings inside too.
As you breathe deeply and just observe them in your heart, the bear always feels warm and fuzzy inside.
Do you?

You feel so special to be here with your animal friends.
They are all so very friendly, kind hearted and snoozy.
Next, the furry fox stops fighting his foxy ways and wisely realizes it is enough exactly as it is.
Together you feel the wisdom inside you that you are enough and perfect exactly as you are.
You let go into a deep sleep.
Your mind switches off and you are almost dreaming away with delight.
Now the soothing squirrel stops squirreling about and becomes very still.
You notice the squirrel's breathing is slower because the squirrel is calm.

You are trusting that there is plenty of everything for everyone.
You relax even more and feel this sense of trust.

There are really no limits and there is so much abundance for all of us.

You start to become still because you are so comfortable here in your perfect sleeping position.

You are on the soft fluffy grass for the night.

Here under the trees is the happiest hedgehog that understands we are all different and that is okay.

It is wonderful.

The hedgehog relaxes its spine to be so friendly and kind.

It is no longer judging itself or judging the animals in the jungle.

They are now accepting them for who they are.

You send love and kindness to yourself and others.

You feel so nice and soft as you melt into a deep sleep.

When you finally stop sleeping and snoozing and dreaming all through the night, you will wake up just like a radiant rabbit tomorrow morning.

You will see the world with fresh eyes because tomorrow is a new day.

Just like the rabbit, you will feel ready to hop about.

You are feeling so calm, confident, and happy inside.

Now the moon is high in the sky above the sleepy jungle.

You know that you are safe and loved here among your animal friends.

Perhaps you are drifting deeper and deeper now into your lovely dreams.
You are loving this beautiful deep sleep here in the calming valley between the peaceful mountains.

Every part of you is now enjoying your deepest and loveliest sleep and it feels brilliant to be a wonderful human being which you already are.
You will snooze and sleep to your heart's content all through the night.

CHAPTER 6

The Magic Unicorn Adventure

Lay down and be still and quiet and peaceful in your bed while you listen.

You can close your eyes if you want to and use your imagination so you can see the story in your mind.

Make sure that everything is comfortable and that you are ready to relax.

A group of three dogs named Bella, Lucy and Jake were on a very special steam train.

They were going on a trip to the seaside.

This train ride was going to take quite a long time.

The dogs thought it was awesome that they were on this magical train.

It made lots of cool sounds as it chugged and chugged along.

It was the best train ever.

The only problem with this train was that it was full. There were no seats to be found anywhere.

The dogs had walked almost halfway through the train and they still couldn't find anywhere to sit.

They came across a cabin which had a very big unicorn standing in the front of the door.

This cabin could not allow dogs inside.

Lucy looked up and said, "hello um would it be alright if me and my sisters can go and sit in there with the unicorns? We can't find anywhere else to sit and this train is full. It would be nice if we can go and sit there."

The giant unicorn just stared down at Lucy and didn't change his face.

He didn't speak, smile or do anything.

Bella said, "he kind of reminds me of one of those guards that stands in front of the palace in London."

Jake says, "oh yeah. You're right he does look kind of intimidating. Do you think he understands us?"

A unicorn inside of the cabin had come to the window.

He slid the door open and said it's okay they can come in and sit with me.

The dogs looked up at the big giant scary looking unicorn who didn't make a single facial expression.

They decided to very slowly and carefully walk around him to get inside the cabin.

When they got inside, the unicorn that had already closed the door sat down on a very comfortable looking pillow.

In fact, the whole cabin was filled with soft plush pillows and blankets.

It looked very comfortable and inviting.

The unicorn introduced himself.

His name is Jack.

He is a prince.

He is very happy to meet you.

The dogs think it is very nice and thinks that it is kind of fancy.

Are you sure you are alright sitting here with us?

I feel like we have to be a royal or something to be sitting next to you.

The unicorn laughed and said, "you don't have to be a royal to be with me. You're very welcome to be next to me. I'm only a prince. That doesn't mean I'm not normal or anything. Does anyone want a chip?"

The prince takes out a bag of chips from his big suitcase and offered the dogs some chips.

When Bella opened the bag of chips a paper snake shot out and scared all the dogs.

They all jumped a little.

The prince thought that it was absolutely hilarious, and he was rolling across from them laughing and holding his stomach.

He thought it was so funny.
The dogs were already getting the idea that this prince was quite funny and had a sense of humor.

The dogs and the prince talked for a while on the train.
They introduced themselves and finding who they were and all about each other.
Unicorns are supposed to have wings, but the prince says he is not old enough to have wings.
His sister Selena has wings and she is a princess.
She is older than I am and better at everything than me.
She is like perfect.
She is kind.
She is sweet.
Jake asked the prince why he is on the train.
Does he have somewhere he needs to go?
The prince is actually on his way home.
He lives in a very special place.
He has been away at boarding school in the city and it is not time for him to go home.
What is boarding school?
Well it is a school where you stay and live there for a while.

Since he is a prince, he has to learn lots of fancy things like how to use the proper fork at the dinner table, how to behave at gatherings, how to speak and how to sit.

The prince said a lot of it is boring and it would be much more fun if he could just learn what you wanted to learn at school rather than learn what everyone else tells you.

Maybe the prince would actually like school but now it is just plain and too boring for him.

He is glad he is going home.

Where does he exactly live?

Through the window of the train came a bright light.

It was the brightest and most beautiful rainbow they had ever seen.

All three of the dogs dropped their jaws all at the same time.

They stared out of the window in awe.

This is the most amazing rainbow they had ever seen.

It was enormous and so so bright.

Each color was really vivid.

It was the most perfect rainbow.

The prince noticed they had seen the rainbow.

He said, "Well since you noticed the rainbow, it means I can tell you where I live. If you can see the rainbow, it means you all have a good heart. If you can't see this particular rainbow, it means you are not a good person and don't have a very loving and kind heart."

The only people that can see this rainbow are the people that live in Unitopia.

Unitopia is the prince's home.

It is a very special place.

The only people who can see the rainbow are people with very good hearts.

If you can see the rainbow, if you can ride on the rainbow, you can go to my home to visit Unitopia.

All three of the dogs decided to visit Unitopia.

But before you visit Unitopia, you must rest first.

You must rest because it the best and most magical place to be.

There is so much to do that you are going to need rest.

Everyone snuggles in together on the lovely pillows.

These pillows feel so nice and at home.

Let's all snuggle down and get really really really comfortable.

Let's all sleep and when you wake up you will be there.

Now close your eyes.

Let's relax.
Just go to sleep.
Prince Jack and the dogs all snuggle together on the big soft fluffy pillows.
They have the smoothest and fluffiest blankets that snuggled you just right.
Everyone closed their eyes and adjusted their bodies.
They got nice and comfortable.
They started to take slower and deeper breaths.
Allowing their bodies to start to relax.
Naturally everything was slowing down.
The sounds of the train were mesmerizing and were calming in the background.
It was quiet in the cabin even though the train was so busy and full.
The guard outside was keeping everyone safe.
They relaxed their paws, hooves and legs.
Their bodies got all heavy and sleepy.
Everyone got very very comfortable.
So comfy and sleepy.
Just moving along on the train tracks listening to the white noise of the train.
Everyone relaxed until eventually they fell asleep.
They all slept for the longest time.

The train made a certain movement and a certain noise that gently woke everyone up.

When they looked out of the window, they saw the fantastic beautiful colored rainbow once again.

It had a sign on it that said, "Unitopia Is This Way."

The dogs and their new friend prince Jack bounced off the train after their long nap.

They were so full of energy and so very excited.

What kind of adventures was waiting for them?

Bella was bouncing all over the place.

All the dogs were excited and couldn't contain themselves.

The rainbow is breathtakingly beautiful.

They all walked over and as they got closer the dogs could tell the rainbow was moving.

As they got closer, they could see that it was like a moving walkway.

The rainbow was moving forwards and upwards.

When they got right in front of it, the rainbow stops for them.

It always stops for you right here until you climb onto it.

Everyone stepped on the rainbow and it started to move again.

They started traveling forward and up this amazing rainbow.

They were going higher and higher.

They all looked down and they could see the trees, the train station, and little tiny houses.

Everything was getting smaller and smaller as they moved higher and higher up this magnificent rainbow.

The dogs never been this high before, but the prince assured them they are completely safe.

You can never get hurt on this rainbow.

It is a very special rainbow so just relax and enjoy the ride and the scenery.

They kept going higher and higher until eventually, it felt like they stopped right at the top of the rainbow.

Then the prince all told them to sit down and slide down the rainbow.

They all started to zoom forwards.

It was the biggest and farthest slide that they had ever seen.

They were all smiling and laughing.

They were all zooming down the other side of the rainbow.

The breeze was blowing in their faces.

Their little whiskers were flying all over the place.

Their noses started to get a little cold as well.

It was amazing and everyone was screaming and laughing.

It was like the best roller coaster they had ever been on and when they finally got to the bottom, there was a giant trampoline.

The prince climbed on it first and was going up so high and back down

High and back down.

Boing.

Boing.

Boing.

Boing.

Then the dogs all jumped on the trampoline as well.

This is the best day in their lives.

Now let's move on and visit the very special unicorns.

There are lots of unicorns that live here.

This place is really really big and it is a special place.

Unitopia is a beautiful place full of hills, trees, bright colored flowers that smelled so sweet, and there were unicorns everywhere all just doing their own thing.

They were all different colors, shapes, and sizes.

It was like a magical dreamland and the three dogs were loving every second of it.

When they got to the palace, they went straight into the throne room.

At the far end of the room was the throne.

You could have probably fit hundreds and hundreds of unicorns in this room.

It was so big and fancy.

There were fancy looking chairs.

On the throne was princess Selena and the King and Queen of Unitopia.

All of a sudden the dogs felt a little nervous.

Jack bowed down and said, "Father. Mother. Selena. These are my new friends. They are special dogs because they have good hearts full of love and they saw the rainbow which means they are obviously very special. I thought it would be really nice if they came to Unitopia and they hung out with me for the day or possibly a sleepover."

The King, Queen and Selena all stood up to greet their guests.

"Welcome is it very nice to meet you." says the King. "You are always welcome here. Have fun and enjoy yourselves. Eat, sleep, play. Whatever you need to do our home is your home for as long as you stay here."

The Queen says, "Yes you're so very welcome. The kitchen is that way if you are hungry after your long journey."

Jack explains to Princess Selena that the dogs would love to meet here and would love to know her more. The princess said, "Of course. I'm so happy that you're here and I have so many things I can show you. I have a whole wardrobe of different clothes if that is something you would be interested in seeing. We can do that sometime in the day but for now, let's go play outside. Let's go play in the back garden and I'll show you all the fun things you can do here." Everyone went out into the garden.

The garden was so beautiful and it was also such a lovely day in Unitopia.
The sun was shining down and the sky was so blue with big white fluffy clouds.
There were different unicorns in different areas of the garden all playing together.
They were all doing their own thing.
Some of them were reading books, some of them were practicing flying, and some of them were creating magic.
They all went to a big giant swimming pool.
Around this swimming pool were enormous trees.
The trees were so tall and so big and so green.
These are really cool looking trees.

Hanging from the trees were long vines hanging down.

The prince went over to one of the vines and ran really fast backwards and forwards on the ground, building up speed and momentum, swung from the vine, and splashed down into the pool.

It was a big splash and water flew everywhere.

Water drenched everyone and the prince thought it was so funny.

Selena said, "well that's my brother for you. He is very kind and very sweet but he also likes to play his little tricks on everyone."

The dogs did not mind at all but they absolutely loved it.

The dogs all grabbed the vine and did exactly as the prince.

They ran all back and forth and just let go and dived into the pool.

Now its time to get something to eat.

Everyone is getting hungry and they all started walking back towards the palace.

As they started to get closer and closer to the palace, they started to hear trumpets playing.

The prince said that trumpets only play when there was a celebration or a gathering of some kind that is happening.

When they opened the door to the palace through these big double doors, there was really loud applause and cheering.

There were hundreds and hundreds of unicorns all gathered in the big throne room.

Everyone is cheering for Jack.

The King comes up to the prince and said to him, "It's time son. We've been watching your actions over the last couple of months and you've grown so much. You are kind, loving, very funny and most of all you're kind and loving. You are very brave and noble. It is time you get your wings."

The prince's jaw dropped.

He just looked shocked.

The King, Queen, and Selena all gathered around the Prince and circled around him so that the prince was standing in the middle of them.

They all put their spiral unicorn horns together and then magic happened.

Gold glitter beams of light cascaded all around Jack.

It made the most amazing sounds.

It sounded like angels singing, harps playing and beautiful sounds of angels floating all over Jack.

These sounds were actually coming from Jack's horn.
Then like magic Jack's wings just unfolded and stretched out really wide.
All the unicorns in the throne room gasped in awe.
Jack's wings were the colors of the rainbow and beautiful blue at the tips.
Even his mane, tail and hooves turned a little blue.
He looks like he is sparkling like the stars.
He starts flapping his rainbow unicorn wings up and down.
He looked the happiest he has ever been.
"Thank you father and mother. Thank you Selena" the prince said as he flapped his wings.
All of the unicorns applauded and stomped their hooves.
They all started singing in celebration.
The three dogs thought it was absolutely amazing.
Unitopia is the nicest place in all of the world.
It is the most nicest place you could possibly go.
Everyone here is so loving, calm, pleasant, and happy.
It is everything you would want in the world.
All of these unicorns are very serene, calm, peaceful, caring, loving, conscious and kind.
It is the nicest place these dogs had ever been too.

Jack wanted to try out his wings and wanted to go outside.

Everyone went outside as the sun was coming down.

There was a warm lovely haze across the land.

It was a beautiful golden light that made your heart warm and glow deep inside.

The princess told the dogs to hop on her back and go for a ride as well.

They all agreed and climbed on her back.

All of a sudden, the prince gracefully started to glide off the ground.

The princess also lifted off the ground and they all started flying up into the sky.

They were flying up in the clouds all over Unitopia.

They saw how beautiful the place was from way up in the sky.

There were hills, valleys, trees and forests.

They could see many different colors from all the flowers below.

They also could see many many different unicorns everywhere.

It was the perfect night for flying.

It was not windy.

It was not cold.

The moon was up in the sky and the beautiful moonlight was shining down on them.

The prince and princess were sparkly brightly in the moonlight.
It was very nice to fly in the sky.
It is so quiet up here.
Eventually it was time to come back down.
Everyone gathered in Selena's room.
It was a very big and special room.
Her bed was enormous made of pink quilt, pink pillows and everything else was white.
It was so very clean and bright.
They all settled down on the princess's large bed and it was really soft and fluffy.
As they all settled down on Selena's soft fluffy bed, the princess started to talk.
Close your eyes and settle down.
Get all snugly under the big soft quilt and think of the amazing day you've just had.
How exciting was it?
Seeing new things and meeting new people.
I know I had a wonderful day meeting Bella, Jake and Lucy.
I want you all to know that you are now my friends.

You are welcome here anytime you wish.

Now all of you take a nice deep breath in and now slowly and gently let it out.
You feel so happy and relaxed.
Remember how high you flew up in the sky?
Remember how lovely that feeling is.
How the wind felt on your face.
Take another deep breathe in and slowly let it out.
When you feel so sleepy.
Now one last time, take another deep breath in and then slowly let it out.
Even though your eyes are closed they feel ever so tired.
You're breathing soft and gently now.
Each time you breathe in you take in the good thoughts and positive feelings.
You're beginning to drift in and out of sleep as you sink deeper and deeper into the lovely soft and squishy quilt.
You smile peacefully to yourself and feel every so happy.
You know that in life, you can be anything you want to be.

You know that you are a truly special person with a loving heart.
You are so loved and you are so protected and you are so very very safe here in Unitopia.

You hear a tapping on the window and you wonder what it could be.
You go over and take a look.
You see a lovely little robin has landed on your window ledge.
He is holding a white envelope in his beak.
He gives it you and flies off.
You open the envelope and you see that it is an invitation with your name on it.
It says we hereby invite you to Unitopia Summer Festival.
It has your name written in fancy golden letters on it.
You are so excited you jump up and down with delight.
Do you remember how to get there?
You have to close your eyes again and breathe in deeply and slowly.
Breath out.
Now breathe in.

Then breathe out.
Breath in and breath out.

Now imagine yourself sitting in a large green field.
The sun is shining brightly, and it is a very beautiful clear day outside.
You can see for miles and miles and miles.
As you look up at the sky you see a beautiful rainbow of all different colors.
The colors are so bright and so clear.
You can see each color in the rainbow.
You recognize this rainbow.
It is the same rainbow to Unitopia!

You go over and you stop at the beginning of the rainbow and it stops moving for you.
You step on it and as soon as you do, it begins to move again.
As it moves forward it also begins to climb higher and higher and higher.
You can touch the colors of the rainbow.
You can feel the colors of the rainbow.
Can you feel them?

The rainbow goes higher still, and you can see the field below you.

Can you see it?

The rainbow now reaches the topmost part and then it begins to move back down again.

It is starting to get a little slippery now so you sit down and you begin to slide.

You are sliding down the rainbow!

It is like a great big waterslide with beautiful colors all around you.

You are going faster and faster!

The wind is whipping through your hair making it fly everywhere.

This makes you laugh out loud and you are laughing so hard your tummy starts to hurt.

You can now see the end of the rainbow and it is coming up fast.

You notice at the bottom of the rainbow is a huge trampoline.

You love this part.

You hit the trampoline so fast you bounce right back up again.

Oh my!

This is so much fun!

You start bouncing some more for a little bit and now you decide to get off the trampoline.

You decide to go search for the summer festival.

As you walk, you instantly see the princess unicorn Selena.
She is with her friends to welcome you back and take you to the summer festival!

She can not wait to show you the amazing summer festival.
She is so happy and delighted you could make it.
You start walking with the princess and her friends.
When you arrive, you hear the sound of wonderful music playing.
There are fairy lights everywhere.
There are also big flashing lights.
You are absolutely amazed by everything you see here.
There are fantastic carnival rides.
Roller coasters are dipping in and out of the clouds.
Unicorn races are happening in the sky.
You can see them flash and run past above you.
This is so fantastic!
There is live music playing and it looks like a gnome is dancing and playing the guitar.
It is a whole band of gnomes!
One is singing in the background; one is playing the drums and one playing the piano.

This is all absolutely wonderful!
There are huge balloons everywhere and so much candy everywhere!
There are so many different carnival games.
There is also a water park!
There are so many different stalls to buy amazing things.
Whatever you want, they have it here at the summer festival.
For a little while more, explore this amazing place with the princess unicorn and her friends.
Go and have lots of fun.
Try all the different games and rides.
Try all of the amazing foods because it smells so yummy.
Spend the rest of the afternoon with your unicorn friends.
Maybe you can find something here to take back home with you.
Maybe something to just remember this amazing day.

Now it is time for you to return home.
It is time for you to leave Unitopia and the wonderful summer festival.

You can always come back next year.
You say goodbye to your friends and return to the beautiful rainbow.
You step aboard and it rises and rises.
You feel so peaceful and relaxed.
You feel so happy and calm and very tired now.
You keep traveling along the amazing rainbow and just thinking about your amazing day.
How wonderful it was to see the princess unicorn and her friends again.
You reach the highest point of the rainbow and you begin to slide down the other side.
You feel so good, happy and sleepy now.
You have had such an amazing day, but it is time for you to sleep.
You are now back in your bed relaxing.
You are back in your warm soft bed.
You can feel your mind is sliding down into a deep deep sleep.

Just rest now and have the best night ever.
You can return anytime you wish.
Now imagine yourself sitting in a large green field.
The sun is shining brightly, and it is such a beautiful clear day.

You can see for miles and miles around you.
You feel very calm and very relaxed and very very peaceful.
You can hear the birds singing to each other.
Can you hear them?

As you look up into the sky you see a beautiful rainbow of many different colors.
The colors are so bright and so clear.
Can you see the beautiful rainbow?
Can you see the colors shining brightly?
The colors look as though they are alive with so much vibrancy and energy.
You are drawn to this rainbow.
When you walk towards it, you feel your steps becoming lighter and lighter.
As you get closer you begin to float, and your feet are not even touching the ground anymore!
Then you realize where you are.
This is the magnificent rainbow to Unitopia!
The rainbow stops moving and you step on it.
Then it starts moving and you begin to climb higher and higher.
You can now touch the colors of the rainbow.
Can you feel it?

As the rainbow goes higher, you can see the fields below you.

You can see the trees and birds flying.

There are a couple of birds flying past you and the rainbow.

When the rainbow reaches the topmost part, you sit down and start to slide.

It is like a such a wonderful colorful waterslide.

There are beautiful colors all around you and you go faster and faster.

The wind is whipping through your hair and making it fly everywhere.

This makes you laugh out loud so much and you are laughing so much it is making your tummy hurt.

You always love this part of the journey to Unitopia.

The end of the rainbow is coming up fast and you can see the huge trampoline.

Then with a great big leap, you bounce off the trampoline and land softly in the beautiful green meadow.

You look around and you can see unicorns everywhere.

They all see you and come to greet you and welcome you back.

They are so pleased that you have come back to vist them again.

They are very magical beings and they always know the truth of things.

They know the truth of you and you are so beautiful to them

All the unicorns speak at once and they say, "Hello! How are you?"

They talk so much that you don't know who to answer first.

Then all of a sudden, they all stop talking and bow their heads to a different unicorn.

This unicorn comes out from the rest of them and she has very silky, very shiny and has a sparkling magical horn.

She is the princess Unicorn and she gives you the biggest smile and says she misses you.

You can see the love in her eyes.

No matter different we may look from each other, she only sees the beautiful person you truly are.

You see her diamond encrusted spiral horn with pink crystals.

You see her beautiful silver mane with sparkles of pink on it.

You can see her sparkling silver hooves as she walks so softly and her hooves make no sound at all.

Her horn is the most powerful out of all the unicorn horns.

She has the strongest one with magical healing qualities.

The gentle breeze of wind blows past her heart and it produces the most beautiful flute like melody.

It sounds so wonderful and soothing to you.

It is so peaceful.

So calming.

The princess tells you that she is glad and so very happy you have come to see her again.

She tells you that this is a very special day.

She says that she has the power to grant you a gift so rare for this one day.

It is a gift no other person has been granted before.

Today she has the power to let you become a unicorn.

She has the power to let you really feel what it is like to be a unicorn.

She asks you if you would like to experience this and you say, "Yes of course!"

The princess unicorn bows one leg and tilts her head towards you and something amazing occurs.

Her beautiful spiral horn begins to shimmer and shine.

Tiny particles of golden dust begin to come from the sky above you and it gently begins to surround you.
It surrounds your whole body and it feels so nice and peaceful.
It is so tingly, warm and relaxing.
Tiny particles of golden dust surrounds all of you.

You feel your body beginning to change.
You feel your legs and arms turning into a unicorn!
Oh my goodness!
You feel a beautiful long tail growing.
A mane that shimmers and shines and then suddenly you feel something happening to your back.
You feel wings growing there.
Oh my goodness!
You have wings and you stretch them out wide.
They feel so fantastic.
The princess smiles happily and graciously to you.
With sparkles coming from her eyes she asks you if you would like to fly with her.
You say oh yes please!
You both turn and gallop together and you begin to fly with each other.
You can feel your wings flapping in the breeze.

You can feel all the muscles in your body moving as one.
Now all of the other unicorns start flying with you as well!
When the princess moves left or right everyone follows her.
It is like all of you have become one.
It is like you guys all are working together.
You can even hear and feel what the other unicorns are feeling and thinking too!
You are completely one with them.
For a few moments, be a unicorn.
Just be a unicorn and fly as a unicorn.
Most of all enjoy what it is like to be one with them.
Feel the breeze on your face and mane.
Be a unicorn.

Now it is time for you to return home.
It is time for you to leave Unitopia.
You gently land back down and as you do, you feel your body return to the normal you.
You feel absolutely amazing.
You feel so grateful for a chance to really fly with the unicorns.
It was so fun to actually be one of them.

You thank the princess for giving you this very special gift today.
You say goodbye to everyone.
You wave and you smile, and you turn to go.
The unicorns teach us to always believe in ourselves.

You feel so sleepy now after your amazing day with the unicorns.
So sleepy now that your eyes have already closed.
You think to yourself that you are so lucky to have such wonderful friends.
You are drifting deeper and deeper now into sleep.
You will have the most wonderful night sleep ever.
Just snuggle down, maybe turn over on your side.
You feel so safe, so protected, and so very very loved.
When you wake up in the morning, you will feel completely refreshed bright and alert.
You feel so very ready to begin the new day.

CHAPTER 7

Great Undersea Friends

Make yourself comfortable.
Lay down on your sofa or bed.
Now tense up all of your muscles and hold it for a few seconds.
Then let it all go allowing your arms and legs to go nice and limp.
Not breath in deeply really filling your lungs with air.
Now breathe out slowly and gently releasing all that air from your lungs.

Breathe in again slowly and deeply.
Hold your breath just for a moment and breathe out.

One more time, deep breathe in and breathe out.
Every time you breathe in, your body becomes more and more relaxed.
Fill your body up.
You are going to feel very loose and very soft as you just breathe in and breath out.
Breathe in and breathe out.

Now imagine you are standing on a beautiful golden sandy beach.
You can hear the wonderful sounds of the waves as they come up onto the sand.
You can even smell the ocean spray.
That lovely ocean spray you can only find at the beach.
You take your shoes off now and your socks.
You start walking on the warm golden sand towards the water and you feel that beneath your feet.
It feels so lovely and so warm.

Now push your toes deep into the sand.
Feel it in between your toes.
Does it feel soft and warm?

Or does it feel big and rough?
You look around you and you realize that the beach is so wide and long.
It stretches out for miles ahead and it is so sunny and warm here.
It is so warm and sunny that it makes you feel so special inside.
You feel so safe and so calm and so peaceful.
You walk over to the water's edge and put your feet in the water.
It feels so nice, so cool and so refreshing.
The water splashes over your ankles just a tiny bit.
Suddenly you hear something behind you.
You turn around and to see what it is.
It is a boy about your age.
He has blonde hair with big blue eyes.
He has the biggest grin on his face too!
He shouts and motions you to come over.
He tells you his name is Adam.
He has come to play soccer on the beach with his friends
He asks if you want to play too.
Well of course you say yes.
You love soccer!
You look around but you do not see anyone else on the beach.

Adam gives a little laugh and tells you he is waiting for his friendly friend the shark.

The shark's name is Henry.

He is Adam's friend and lives in the sea.

He is not just an ordinary shark. He is actually a magical shark.

Adam reaches in his pocket for a whistle.

This is a magical whistle that he uses to call Henry.

Henry has a very good sense of hearing.

He can hear this whistle from miles away.

Adams puts the whistle to his mouth and gives it a big blow.

Henry will be here soon Adam says.

You suddenly see a fin pop up just above the waves.

Then you see Henry's head pop up and looks really big in the waves!

You hope Henry is not hungry now.

You wonder how on earth are you going to play soccer with a shark?

They do not have any feet.

You look at Henry and he has sparkling magical dust floating around him all over in the water.

It looks so amazing but you can't seem to see where it is coming from.

Then the most astonishing thing happens.

Henry walks out of the water with two legs and two feet!

Your mouth drops wide open.
A shark is walking on the beach out of the water!
He is also wearing bright yellow shorts and soccer shoes.
Adam tells you he only grows legs when you come on land and especially to play soccer, but when he goes back into sea he will turn back into a normal shark.
Adam tells you he doesn't eat people so don't worry.
Henry actually loves fruits and vegetables!

Henry puts on his goggles and says alright, let's play some football!
You will be on offense and Adam can play on defense and Henry will be the goalkeeper.
For a few moments, you play soccer with Henry and Adam.
Just have fun on this wonderful golden sandy beach.
See if you can try score some goals.

Wow! That was so fun!
Did you score a goal?
Henry asks if you would like to meet his brother Bruce.

Well of course you say yes.
Henry tells you can ride on his back in the sea and just hold onto his fin underwater.
He says he has spare goggles for you to put on.
He then sprinkles you with golden magic dust.
This is so you can breathe underwater!
You are absolutely amazed by this!
Harry swims far out into sea and dives down deep into the water.
You can see fish swimming past you.
One of them takes off his little cup and says good morning and swims off.
You see all of the underwater sea creatures just all floating and swimming around.
What else can you see down here?
What can you see under the water?
Then you see a house underwater.
It is Henry's house!
This is where he lives and Bruce is waiting at the doorway.
Bruce gives a big grin and says hello to you.
He asks if you would like to have a strawberry smoothie.
You go inside and you say hello to his mom and dad.
The dad's name is Will and his mom's name is Emma.

You finish your smoothie and Bruce suggests that you show you around where they live.

Maybe some of their other friends will be out playing as well.

You meet their crab friend named Dotty.

She is such a friendly crab.

She is sitting on a rock knitting with bright pink yarn.

She is wearing glasses perched on the end of her nose.

She tells you she is knitting a scarf to go with her brand new hat.

Henry tells you that Dotty is his best friend.

They go everywhere together.

She is also teaching Henry to knit.

Just for a little while, go see and explore with Henry, Bruce and Dotty.

Maybe you guys can play volleyball.

Dotty loves that.

Maybe you can just swim around to your heart's content.

Whatever you want to do you can make happen in this magical underwater place.

Now that you have seen where all your new friends live, Henry asks if you would like to stay at his house tonight.
In fact, he says everyone can.
How wonderful!
You get to have a sleepover with a very friendly shark with all his friends and family too.
Go back to Henry's house and you all go into his bedroom.
To your surprise, there is a bed for everyone.
Dotty finds herself the softest bed and climbs on it.
You all find your own beds and settle down nicely.
You do feel rather sleep now.
You had a pretty amazing day playing soccer with Adam and a shark that can grow legs.
Your eyes begin to feel very heavy and very sleepy now.
Your eyelids are beginning to droop.
Your body feels so peaceful, so relaxed, so calm and so very very heavy now.
You feel ever so happy.
You close your eyes and just listen to the sounds of the ocean.
You feel your breathing as it begins to slow down.
Your chest is gently rising and falling.
You take a deep breath in gently and slowly breathe out.

Listen to the gentle sounds of the ocean.
It is time for you to rest for a beautiful restful sleep.
You go deeper and deeper into sleep.
When you wake up in the morning, you will be back in your very own bed.

CONCLUSION

Thank you so much for listening to *Bedtime Sleep Meditations For Children.*

I hope this book has helped you have lots of wonderful dreams and amazing nights of sleep.

If you ever find yourself stressed out, angry, overwhelmed or sad, you can always refer to this book's teachings and re-listen to it again.

If you enjoyed this book and if it has helped you have a better night's sleep, be sure to leave a thoughtful review on Amazon of how this book has helped you. This is so more kids like you can have amazing sleeps every night!

Thank you again for listening to this book and I wish you all the love, happiness and amazing nights of sleep ahead!

www.ingramcontent.com/pod-product-compliance
Lightning Source LLC
Chambersburg PA
CBHW072002110526
44592CB00012B/1181